ASPHALT HUNTER

TOM BRINER

NEWMAN SPRINGS PUBLISHING
320 Broad Street
Red Bank, NJ 07701

First originally published by Newman Springs Publishing 2022

ISBN 978-1-63881-697-3 (Paperback)
ISBN 978-1-68498-029-1 (Hardcover)
ISBN 978-1-63881-698-0 (Digital)

Printed in the United States of America

Prologue

I Hate Perry County

I had a pretty straightforward repo order on a newer Ford truck. The order even said the debtor was expecting me. Sounds easy, right? You see, there are two types of repos: voluntary and not voluntary. The order said it was neither.

It was dark when I got down to the city of Shawnee, Ohio, in Perry County. Did I say how much I hated Perry County? You see, it is not really a city anymore; it is more of a ghost town. Look it up. Of course, the truck wasn't in town. It was out in the hills, on some fucking dirt farm with narrow winding gravel roads. I finally arrived, and there it sat, about fifty yards from the house, with its ass end out. *This will be an easy hook and go,* I thought.

It started easy enough. There was a full moon, and it was a nice evening, so bright you did not even need a flashlight. I backed up to the truck, got out, and took my time hooking it up. I even noticed a key lying on the dash. Remember, the owner was expecting me. Just as I got it lifted, I heard a door slam. I looked up, and two guys were heading toward me, yelling, "Sit it down! Sit it down!" They were pissed. They got right in my face, calling me every name in the book.

The older guy, around forty, decided to take a swing, and it was a haymaker I could see coming. I took a step back, put my hand on the bumper of his truck and the other hand on the back of my tow truck, lifted myself up, and planted a foot right in his chest. Down he went into the gravel. Soon his son was next to the party. I jumped over the wheel lift to get some separation, but his son didn't realize it was there. He tripped and went face-first down on the ground. I then jumped in my truck and took off.

I thought I was clear, heading back down the winding road. About a minute later, I realized the old man had jumped in the driver's side of the truck I was towing. He then started the truck and tried to drive off of the wheel lift. Now during all the excitement, I didn't strap down the rear tires, but I did have deep pans on my wheel lift that wrapped around part of the tires. He kept his foot on the brakes, so I was dragging him down the narrow winding road with a deep gully on the left side. I just needed to make it back to town, so I kept on pulling this asshole.

Soon his son appeared right beside me in a car, and he was trying to run me off the road. He finally got in front of me and turned the car sideways, but I was not stopping. I T-boned the kid and pushed him right over the side of the gully, and down he went. It must have slowed my truck down enough that good old Dad was able to get his truck in four-wheel drive, and he drove off my wheel lift, leaving his bumper behind.

During this whole time, I was on my Nextel phone (remember those?), trying to get help. I finally got a hold of my buddy Tod, who called the cops. When I got into the town of Shawnee, I was stopped by a cop who drove a Cruiser that had to be twenty years old, and he had mustard stains on an old wrinkled uniform. I explained everything that happened, and all he said was "Well, they called first." Really, they called first! Now that is some expert police work. Never mind them trying to kick my ass or run me off the road.

When I checked in at the office the next day, the guy had turned in the truck at Park National Bank, and guess who got charged for the bumper? If you get a chance, look up Shawnee. It is a real shithole. Did I mention I hate Perry County?

To My Parents and Family

Sorry, Dad. I know you always wanted the best for me. You wanted me to get a regular job with benefits, have a family, and live the American dream. I think you knew only part of that was going to happen. Dad, I was listening to you the whole time. I hung on to every word. You only thought I wasn't listening. I remember everything, and I try to teach the same lessons to my kids. In the end, I hope I made you proud.

Mom, sorry about making you worry. I know a large part of your gray hair was my fault. Thanks for believing in your little boy. You would be so proud of Brittani. I can still see you two sitting on the couch, doing word searches and watching craft and cooking shows. Now I know where she gets it. I miss you both.

Melanie, I love you. You are definitely my better half. I am blessed to have you in my life. I know you have chronic pain, and I wish I could make it disappear. I hope you love your life in Florida; the best times are yet to come.

To Rachel and Charlie, I am so proud of you both. I love our family vacations and hope to do many more. I loved watching you grow up and run track and cross country. Charlie, being an officer in the Navy suits you. You're a born leader; always trust your judgment. Rach, I am glad you found something you love to do. Being a pharmacy tech looks good on you, and the sky is the limit for you. I love being part of your life.

Brittani, well, this is your dad's crazy life. I know you never realized what I did for a living and the things I got into, but this should bring you up to speed. You have had two great role models in your life, Holly and Melanie, and it doesn't get better than that. It probably drives them crazy that we are so much alike. Stubbornness, determination, adventurism, and by God, when we are right, *we are right*—just to name a few. I wish I had been around more when you were growing up, but I did the best I could. I missed the little things, like watching you get on the bus, being there for your first day of school, or playing pitch and catch, like my dad did with me. You have made me so proud.

Well, this is it—my story and your legacy.

My Hometown

I lived in the small town of Ontario, Ohio, right beside Mansfield. It sits between Cleveland and Columbus, Ohio. It was a great place to grow up, and you couldn't find a more middle-class town. My mom was a cook at the school, and my dad was a supervisor at Columbia Gas. I had great parents. I had a sister, but we were never very close. She had a good heart but got caught up in the bad things in life and passed way too early.

My childhood and school years were awesome. I did average in school, C+, B- average, but I loved sports. I loved playing basketball and running track. I also played football, and it was probably my best sport; I just didn't get into it as much. I even played for the Shelby Blues semi pro football team for a season. I had a few offers to play college basketball at Baldwin Wallace and Eastern Kentucky, but at the time, I just didn't want to be in school anymore.

I always wanted to own my own business, like a restaurant. I never did own a restaurant. I worked at a few factories, built windows, and did a few other jobs. Then in the late seventies and early eighties, the economy bottomed out. I picked up my stuff and moved to Clearwater, Florida. On my second day in Florida, I found a job. I was the security guard at the Madeira Beach Yacht Club. I was tall and had blond hair, and the owner said I would look good at the front gate.

I found a place to live, a little bungalow right on the beach. Could you ask for more than that as a young man from Ohio? That night, I went to my aunt's house for dinner. She lived in Largo. When I returned home and turned on the lights, I got a big surprise—*roaches*, hundreds of them. More roaches than in a horror movie. That night, I slept in my truck and moved the next morning.

I ended up in Clearwater and loved being by the water. I saved my money by buying one pizza a week and eating a slice or two every day. Besides work, I didn't have much to do, so I would run along the water each day; I was in good shape. Soon I had enough money to buy a lawn service, and then I was off to the races. I worked hard, and my customers loved me and my work ethic. (Thanks, Dad.) Soon that business grew to servicing one hundred lawns and a few commercial accounts.

I was dating a girl from Ontario, Holly Houck, and she was getting ready to graduate from Ohio State University. Soon after we married, we purchased the house across the street from where I was living. It was the house of a lawn customer. I was not the highest bidder at the time, but he sold it to us anyway. Thank you, Mr. Spivey. (I told you my customers loved me.)

As time went on, I bought out more lawn services and purchased more rental properties. Florida was the place to be. If I still owned all the properties I did then, I would be a multimillionaire today. Lawn work is hard work in Florida; ninety-degree days and the humidity will kill you. After seven years, it was starting to wear on me, and I was looking to make a change. Now after all this, how did a small-time middle-class guy get into the repo and bail bonds business?

Getting into This Crazy Business

I guess I should first start by telling you how I got into this crazy business. I was playing basketball in an adult league in Clearwater, Florida, when I was approached by a man who said, "Hey, how would you like to play college ball?" I told him I was almost thirty years old, and his reply was "I can work with that." Soon I was traveling around the country, showing coaches my skills. Now don't get me wrong, I am no Michael Jordan, but I could shoot the ball. Soon the offers started to come in, and I chose a school in Minnesota—not a great choice, by the way. So now I was in college for the first time at age thirty and playing basketball. If that is not crazy enough, I started my college days, and after a year, I realized cold-ass Minnesota was not for me. Also, the coach and I didn't see eye to eye.

My wife, Holly, was offered a position with the Defense Department in Columbus, Ohio, so we moved to Newark, Ohio, where I could go to school and play ball, and my wife could commute to work. Needing a flexible job, I started looking for work. I noticed a position open for a repo man in my area, with an emphasis on experience, of which I had none. But what does a good repo man do? He improvises. I called and got an interview, where I proceeded to lie my ass off. It must have worked, because a couple of days later, they offered me the job. At the time, they said I could make $500 a week. In the early nineties, that was not bad money.

They sent me out with a guy named Cecil for training, and our first repo was insane. We pulled up to the house and blocked in the truck, and Cecil hit the door (knocked). The guy was not happy to see us. Cecil explained the order to the guy and told him he could get his personals out of the truck, which he did in spectacular fashion. You see, he was a contractor, and his truck was full of tools. He jumped up on the bed and started cussing and throwing everything out on the driveway—and I mean throwing. Saws, routers, table saws, ladders, boxes of fifty-pound nails that hit the driveway and exploded like a bomb. He was going nuts, and he was not a happy camper. To add insult to injury, Cecil then asked him for the keys, which he gave to Cecil at about 90 mph to the chest. Cecil turned to me and said, "Welcome to the repo business." He and I picked up two more cars that night, with less fanfare, thank God.

I must admit, I thought about giving it up after that night, but I didn't. In fact, I brought my best friend into the business the next month when they were in need of more help in Northern Ohio, and together, we set the company record for the most repos that month. His name was Tod Duffner, and I will refer to him many times in the following pages.

Tod and I had a talent for this type of work, and soon we became private investigators, finding cars no one else could find. With the help of Tracy, one of our office skip tracers, we were unbeatable. Tracy could find anyone and anything. She was the best skip tracer in the business. Tracy would go on to own her own repo business and is still in the business today. She has outlasted all of us. You see, the trick of repossessions is to find the car without emptying your fuel tank looking for it, so phone work is critical. We ran every scam there was to make sure our debtor was home or at work. For instance, we would call and ask for the debtor and say that we were from a delivery service and that the package needed a signature. Who is not excited about getting a mysterious package? We would say the bank needed an inspection done on the car because it had a recall notice. We would call and say we had gone to school with the debtor and wanted to see our old friend; when would he be home? If the car had a "For sale" sign on it, we would take it for a test drive and not return.

But the best place to repo a car is at the person's workplace. First of all, if you have your own tow truck, you just hook it up and go, no keys needed. If you need the keys, you just ask for the person at the business; they will be so embarrassed they'll hand you the keys and worry about their personal property later.

Soon Tod and I were pulling down $1,000 a week each. In fact, we were so good at finding people that a local bail bond agent wanted to hire us. So soon after passing our state insurance test, we were off doing fugitive recovery and writing bail bonds. The following are some of our crazy adventures.

Rules of Repo

1. Never say anything bad about the bank.
2. Never knock on a door after 9:00 p.m.
3. Don't breach the peace.
4. The police can't help you take the car.
5. Don't enter a closed garage or locked unit.
6. Get in and out ASAP. The longer you're there, the more can go wrong.
7. Don't make any promises you can't keep. It will come back to bite you in the ass.

Fly Wagon

Some people are just pigs. Who would spend thousands of dollars on a car just to fill it with trash? Now believe me, I am no neat freak, far from it. Just ask my wonderful wife. At any time, if you look in my truck, you will find an empty pop bottle, a slushy cup on the floor, and even a sandwich wrapper or two. But some people take it to another level.

Tod and I had a voluntary repo in Newark, Ohio, and I had made contact with the woman a day earlier. She told me that she had removed everything she wanted from the car and that the keys would be above the visor. We pulled up to the house, which was in a nice neighborhood. Tod jumped out to drive a nice-looking Ford Taurus wagon. As he opened the door, I noticed him take a step back from the car, and I yelled out, "What's wrong?"

He replied, "This thing stinks."

Nevertheless, he jumped in like a trooper, and off we went, back to my house. We often stored cars at my place because I had the room. When we had several, we would then run them over to Columbus Fair Auto Auction. When we arrived at my house, he shot out of the car like a man possessed, remarking again how the car stunk. I even saw a mouse jump out behind him. I went over to the car and looked inside it. The car was full of trash. Anything you would put in your trash can was in there; food wrappers, half-full coffee cups, soda bottles, rotten food, and anything you can think of was in that car. We rolled up the windows and locked it. We then headed off to look for more cars.

A few days later, we gathered up a few friends, and we were going to drive several cars to Columbus. When Tod pulled in, he said, "I am not driving the stink wagon." I just started laughing and didn't think much of it. Everyone grabbed keys and headed toward their car. My wife at the time, Holly, got in our Buick so we all would have a ride back home from the auction. I then headed over to get in the stinky car. I knew it would be unpleasant, but I had no idea how bad it had gotten. The sun had baked that car for four days.

I opened the door, and the biggest cloud of flies started to come out. I am not kidding. It was a black cloud. It was followed by a mess of mice that had made a home under the seats. For several minutes, we all stood back in amazement as more and more flies and mice came out of that car. Just as I thought the car was empty, one last fat mouse appeared on the bottom of the door frame, stood up and gave us a nod like he was saying thanks, and ran off into the vacant lot next door. Needless to say, no one drove that car to the auction. We towed it.

The Groper

Funny but sad is the only way to explain this repo. One evening, I asked a friend at the college to go with me to pick up a couple of cars in the Columbus area. I would ask people to go with me because I could only tow one car at a time, and having an extra driver is always helpful.

The first car belonged to a dancer at a strip club. So we headed there first, of course. My friend asked if his brother could ride along, and I said, "Sure, why not?" When I showed him the order, he said he knew a girl at the club. We arrived at the club, and he spoke to the bouncer at the door and asked for his friend. As you can see, I am not using names in this story. (Too embarrassing.) The young lady arrived. She was a tall good-looking girl, and she was very nice. I go for the short brunette girls myself. Anyway, the girl we were looking for was not working yet.

As we were standing at the door, another girl walked up to the first girl and said, "It's your turn to sit with the groper." We all started laughing. She told us this guy comes in three nights a week and gets real handsy with the girls, but he was a good tipper. She went on to further explain how foul the guy was.

We all wanted to get a look at him. She took us down the hallway and pointed him out to us. The two brothers turned white as a sheet, turned, and ran out of the place.

I walked out after them, and one had his hands on his knees, breathing like he just ran five miles. The other was leaning over the side of my truck. All I could say was "What the hell is going on?"

At the same time, they yelled, "That's our *dad*!"

I then said, "Well, at least he's a good tipper." That didn't go over well.

PS. The car we were looking for showed up twenty minutes later. Easy repo.

Tarred and Feathered

Tod and I received a notice from the court that we had an FTA (failure to appear) on a bond we wrote. So we knew we had to find this guy in short order; the judge was never too kind to bondsmen, and $5,000 was on the line.

We first went to his given address and found out that he had moved a month earlier. Strike 1—he did not let us know. The next address was his girlfriend's house. We knocked on the door several times before she answered. After a short conversation at the door, we knew she was covering for him. Strike 2. So we asked permission to search the house. She said no and asked if we had a warrant. Strike 3.

Bondsmen don't need warrants if we have a good suspicion the person is hiding there. We quickly pushed by her as she stood screaming at us. Tod headed upstairs, and I searched the first floor. Neither one of us had any luck. I asked Tod if he looked in the attic, and he said no. So off we went to the attic.

We opened the hatch, and the attic appeared to be empty, just full of blown-in insulation. As we shone our flashlights all around, we saw a large lump of insulation at the very back. Not wanting to crawl into a hundred-degree attic, I decided to throw something at the lump. I removed a battery from the flashlight and gave it a good toss. As the battery hit the lump, out jumped our boy. He was sweating like a pig and covered in sticky insulation from head to toe. All we could do was laugh.

On the way out of the attic, he missed a support beam, and one of his legs went right through the drywall. When we got him outside and cuffed, he asked if we could hose him off, which we did.

When we arrived at the city jail, the jailer asked what the hell happened. As we explained, all he did was shake his head and smile.

Backwoods Repo

Tod and I went to Zanesville, Ohio, to repo a truck that we were told was stuck out in the woods somewhere. We hit the kid's front door and asked him where the truck was parked. He told us he had it stuck about a mile back in the woods, and no one could get it out. He had even called a towing company to get it out, and they were unsuccessful. That's all Tod had to hear—that no one could get it out.

The kid gave us directions and the keys, and we headed out. We arrived at the location and decided to walk the trail to find the truck. After walking through a mud trail and swamp water for about forty minutes, we finally came upon an S-10 pickup backed up against a fallen dead tree, and it was buried in the mud.

After some time, we came up with a plan. I would wedge myself between the truck and the tree and push with my legs against the tree and my back against the tailgate. Then Tod would put it in four-wheel drive and give it hell. Little by little, we moved the truck, mud flying everywhere and covering me from head to toe.

Finally, we hit a dry patch, and the truck started to move. I yelled at Tod and told him to keep going, and he started flying through the woods. About every fifty feet, there was another huge mudhole, a high spot, and then another mudhole. This continued for a mile.

What Tod didn't realize was that I was still holding on to the tailgate, with my feet on the bumper, and I looked like a rodeo rider, holding on for my life. Tod was driving like a madman, hitting these mudholes full force, and the truck felt like it was going airborne on every rise.

As we neared the woods' end, Tod slammed on the brakes. My knees hit the top of the tailgate, and I did a complete flip into the bed of the truck, landing flat on my back. Tod jumped out of the truck, and his eyes were as big as dinner plates. He had no idea I had been hanging on for dear life. We looked at each other for about fifteen seconds and then burst out laughing.

We were so proud of ourselves we even drove back to the kid's house and let him clean out his personal property. I think Tod just wanted to show that kid that somebody could get that truck out—us.

Big Bonds

Big bonds are always nice to write. It does not take much more effort to write a big bond than a small one. The difference is collateral and whether the person is a flight risk. The biggest bond I wrote was $250,000. Of that bond, $12,500 went in my pocket, and $12,500 went to the head office. All bond companies work on different percentages. I received 5% of the 10% of each bond I wrote. As long as the bond was approved by the home office, I was not on the hook if the person didn't show up for court.

Some bondsmen make more, and some make less; it all depends on how much skin in the game you want to be responsible for if the person is a no-show. My $250,000 bond was for money laundering. When my client was raided by the Feds, he had a million dollars in his freezer. My collateral was his beautiful home and business. He showed up for court.

I also had Detroit drug dealers walk in my office and drop $25,000 cash on my desk in a grocery bag. Those bonds I passed. I don't want to spend a week in Detroit chasing down people with gang ties and guns they are not afraid to use.

I did have an interesting bond with a massage parlor owner one time in Mansfield, Ohio. Good ole Mansfield had a massage parlor that was constantly put out of business by Mansfield Police. But as soon as it closed, another would open in the same building. One of those owners called me one day and asked to meet at the courthouse. He had four Asian girls who had been arrested, each with $10,000 bonds.

I walked in, and he was sitting outside the clerk's office, waiting for me. I was a bit surprised when I saw him. He must have been in his seventies. I told him the cost of the bonds and started to pull out the paperwork. He then said, "*No paperwork.*" I told him it was a must, and again he said, "*No paperwork.* I will pay cash." He then opened up his briefcase and showed me stacks of cash, a whole brief-case full.

Now I am an honest man, and I told him he didn't need me. He could simply walk into the clerk's office and post the bond himself. A lot of people don't realize this fact. Many bondsmen won't tell you that, and that makes this profession look bad. I hate some of the shady people in this business, and Mansfield had one of the worst.

The older gentleman said he didn't want his name on anything, and he proceeded to count out $40,000 right out of his briefcase. When the girls were released, I still needed their information and phone numbers. When they finished, I looked over their paperwork and was surprised to see that a couple of the women were in their sixties. But let me tell you, they didn't look a day over thirty. Asian women must age very well.

About a week later, all the women showed up for court, and I refunded the older gentleman's money, minus my 10%—$4,000.

Fat Man in Findlay

We were out late one evening trying to find a car at a prison. We were not there very long when a roving patrol spotted us and chased us off the property. As we left, we got a call from one of the girls at our office. She told us we needed to pick up a car in Findlay ASAP.

As we pulled up in Tod's Toyota truck, I jumped out to check the VIN (vehicle identification number). It matched, and the keys were in the ignition. I motioned to Tod to start the car, and we were off. About twenty minutes down the road, we received a call from the office, and the girl who told us to take the truck said that she had made a mistake and that the owner had paid off the car that day. She then told us to take the car back but to be careful, because the owner was pissed. We headed back to drop off the car.

When I pulled into the drive, the owner ran out of the house like he had been shot from a gun. He was a mountain of a man, and he was only wearing boxer shorts. He got up in my face and, with his fists clenched, started swearing at me, wanting to pound me into the ground. He then stated that he wanted gas money for the time we drove his car. That was not going to happen.

I told him that I had no cash on me, but Tod did. I walked to the driver's side door of Tod's truck and told him what this dude said. The car owner then opened up the passenger door on Tod's truck and started swearing at him.

I whispered to Tod to floor it, and I would simply outrun this big man. Well, he floored it, and this guy held on to the door frame of Tod's truck. Now imagine a three-hundred-pound man hanging on to a truck going about 40 mph, flapping around like a flag. All I could do was run after the truck.

Finally, the fat man let go, and believe it or not, he landed on his feet and started running full speed. He then realized I was still behind him, as he started to slow down. I ran by him like a jet. He then started chasing me down the road. This guy's bare feet were hitting the pavement so hard it sounded like he had swim fins on.

The big man could run, but I soon heard him gasping for air. I knew I had him. As I was running, I reached back, flipped him the bird, and said, "Run, fat boy, run!" He then gave up, and when I looked back, he was bent over with his hands on his knees, gasping for air.

I caught up with Tod at the end of the street and jumped in his truck, and the first thing he said was "Let's go to Burger King," like nothing had happened.

Buddha Belly

This repo was definitely memorable. The bank had a rush order on the repo and was willing to pay $400 for this van. Apparently, a couple other companies had tried to pop the guy but were chased off by him and his dog.

At the time, if you had the VIN of the car, you could get a key cut right from the dealership, so that's what we did. We headed to Frazeysburg, Ohio. The guy lived on top of a hill, and his driveway went straight up to his house. He could see anyone coming from a long way away.

So I came up with a plan. I would crawl up the side of the hill from the backside of the property, jump in the van, and take off. Sounds easy, right? Well, the hill was full of every type of briar you could think of, so by the time I made it up, I was bleeding. To top it off, his dog was chained near the van. All I could do was make a dash for the van and hope the door was not locked. The chain on the dog gave me about two feet to get in and go, and that's what I did.

After I hit the road and made it a couple of miles, a pickup passed me at a high speed and suddenly slid sideways and blocked the road. And then it happened. A man of about four hundred pounds jumped out and held his arms out for us to stop. He was naked from head to toe, with the biggest Buddha belly you have ever seen. Luckily, we had enough room to drive around him as he beat his fists on the van.

We drove to the police department and reported the repo, which is the law in Ohio. The debtor had already reported it stolen. Not stolen, just repossessed.

Double Bagger

Tod and I were looking for a guy in Newark, Ohio, who had jumped bond. Well, after months of running leads, we found him living in a craphole of a trailer out in the country.

He was not home, but I played his answering machine while I helped myself to a Pepsi out of his fridge. Well, the machine told us when he would be meeting someone at his trailer to sell his motorcycle. And where was his motorcycle? In the bedroom of his trailer. We then realized, after a call to the office, that his bike was also out for repo.

We staked out his trailer for four hours, and when he arrived, we cuffed him up with very little trouble. The side door of the trailer was directly across from the bedroom where his bike was parked. After about thirty minutes of removing the steps up to the door, we were able to pull the pickup right to the side door. Tod then jumped on the Harley Sportster and rode the bike out of the bedroom into the back of his truck.

We called that the great double bagger.

The Saddest Repo

I was sent a repo order to pick up a car in Newark, Ohio, and I noticed the debtor worked at the DMV. Now who has not stood in line for hours at the DMV and watched the employees goof around and take their good old time before helping you? Well, this was my chance at a little payback, I thought.

Like most repo orders, it gave me a home address, work address, three references, and other information the bank thought relevant. So that evening, I headed out to the home address, and sure enough, the car was sitting there, pretty as a picture. It was even backed in, so I could back right up to it and get it on the hook.

After I hooked it up and lifted it up a foot or two, I hit the door. It was right at 9:00 p.m., so it was still legal to do so. Just so you know, you can't knock on a door after 9:00 p.m.

The lady came out and was in a bit of shock. I explained the order to her and told her she could get her personals out of the car. (I will explain the rules on personals later.) She started to beg me not to take the car and said that she could make the payment tomorrow. I explained that I had to follow the bank's instructions. Her little boy had come out of the apartment and was holding on to his mom's hand, listening to the whole conversation. She continued to beg me as she was cleaning out the car. Soon her little boy ran back into the apartment and disappeared for a few minutes.

She finally cleaned out her car, and I was removing the tags for her, when I felt a tug on my shirt. I looked down, and to my surprise, her little boy was standing there with outstretched arms, holding his piggy bank. Did I mention the tears running down his cheeks? At that moment, I hated my job, and my big plan for revenge on the DMV worker was a complete bust.

I didn't repo another car that night. I just drove home and went to bed. I sure hope that kid is successful in life and can buy his mom the car of her dreams, because he was willing to at age three.

How Personals Work

This was my favorite part of the job. When a car is repossessed and the owner does not clean it out, they are sent a letter by the repo company telling them they have thirty days to do so. Each agent, after the repo, must clean out the car, bag or box everything up, and date it with the debtor's name. Yes, it's a bit of a pain, but I was smart about it and was able to turn it into more money.

After the thirty days, the personals would be headed to a dumpster, or that agent could keep it. You would be surprised what people keep in their car. Let's put it this way: I had three garage sales a year and made thousands of dollars on tools, DVDs, clothes, books, electronics, and sporting equipment. I even found an AR-15, which I turned in to the local police. Some repo guys never bothered to even go through people's personal property, but I made it a bonus.

Cop Gone Bad

I received a repo order close to my house, about a mile away, which was always a nice thing. The only problem was, the order was for a Columbus police officer's Mustang.

I drove by his house, and there it was, sitting in the garage with the garage door open, which was very important. You see, if the garage door is open, the car is fair game. You can never open a garage door; that would be breaking and entering. I decided to play it cool and hit the door and talk to him first. I told him that his car was out for repo and asked if he would voluntarily turn it over to me. Of course, he said no and told me he knew several people at our office and was even dating one of our tracers. Oh, he was also married. He told me that he had to leave for work soon and that I needed to leave. He would make his payments tomorrow.

I left for about ten minutes and drove by again. His car was still in the same spot, but the trunk was open and his police gear and bag were sitting behind his car. I wasn't driving my tow truck at the time, so I parked my car a street over. I slowly approached the garage from his blind side and entered it. I looked in the car and saw that his keys were in the ignition, so I threw his stuff in the trunk, including his service weapon; got in the car; and drove off. I started to head back to my house when, all of a sudden, a piece-of-crap station wagon tried to run me off the road.

It was the cop, driving his housekeeper's car. It didn't take much to lose him in that piece of crap, and I drove it home.

Soon I was called to the Newark Ohio Police Department, with them saying they needed to talk to me. When I arrived at the station, an officer met me, and the debtor was with him. The Newark cop started asking me for my info and wanted my driver's license. He then read my info out loud, right in front of his fellow cop, telling him where I lived. He then put me in a holding room and let the debtor leave. Can you see the setup coming? They held me for about an hour until my attorney called them. Surprise, surprise, when I arrived home, the Mustang was gone.

I hate dirty cops, but my revenge would be swift. I found out about a week later that the cop (debtor) was arrested for robbing a jewelry store he had been guarding after hours. I also came to find out that he had a gambling problem and had been stealing things all over town. Hope he had a good time in prison. Oh, also, his wife divorced him.

Garage Doors

One of the first things you learn about when repossessing cars is garage door dos and don'ts. And what about carports? First thing you should know is, looking in the garage is okay as long as you don't open any doors—main doors or garage doors. Never open a garage door to get to a car. That is a B&E. Carports are okay because there is no garage door. You can simply walk right up to the car; no barrier is involved. So what about an open garage door? That's a little bit of a gray area, but most agree that an open garage door is the same as a carport; the car is fair game.

That takes me to a repo in Pataskala, Ohio. Tod and I had been looking for a Windstar minivan, and we knew exactly where it was. It was always in the garage of the debtor's home. We could never catch them out and about in it, and it was never seen at the workplace. Every night, they would crack the door on the garage open about a foot so the cats could run in and out at night. It was so frustrating to be able to see a repo but not be able to get it. This went on for months. Our boss even told us about a device you could buy that would scan garage door codes and open doors. We declined that route.

Anyway, one evening, we happened to drive by the house, and the garage door was open. We had a key already made for the van, so I ran up to the van. Off we went. We headed back to Newark to do the paperwork and clean out the personals.

Now I am not sure whose jurisdiction this was, Pataskala PD's or the Licking County sheriff's, but soon we found ourselves sitting in the Newark Police Department's holding room again. The first thing they did was separate Tod and I. For the next hour, they accused us of opening a garage door. They asked question after question on how we opened the garage door, telling us we could be charged at any time, blah, blah, blah. This officer kept slamming his hand on the desk, saying, "We know you opened the door. Make it easy on yourself. I wonder what your buddy is telling us." You would have thought we committed the crime of the century.

Soon they kicked us free; neither one of us would ever squeal on the other. It's the code.

I will never understand how we were pulled in by Newark Police when we were ten miles out of their jurisdiction. Somehow the debtor was connected to the Newark PD.

Muskingum County Sheriff

Tod and I didn't always work together; he also had his own tow truck. Sometimes when we had keys, we didn't use our trucks at all. Tod worked the northern part of Ohio, and I did the central and some southern counties. Sometimes when I needed help, I would ask one of the college kids at the Ohio State Newark campus to help me out. This story is one of those times.

I had a repo down around Zanesville, Ohio, and I asked one of the guys in the law enforcement class to ride along. The kids always jumped at the chance to go. As we pulled up to the debtor's house, he came out in short order. It was about 10:00 p.m., and he knew why we were there. He was a nice man; he already had the car cleaned out, and he handed us another set of keys.

Then all of a sudden, a dozen cruisers and cops on four-wheelers were all over this man's farm. They told us that two guys had just assaulted a deputy and knocked him into a ditch. It was hunting season at the time, and the deputy was just checking their licenses. Apparently, they were on foot in the area, and the cops told us to just hang tight. After about thirty minutes of the cops searching the woods with high-powered lights, four-wheelers, and many on foot, they gave up.

I looked at my partner at the time (I remember his last name was Saterfield) and said, "Let's have some fun." We got in our cars and drove about a half mile up the road, where there was a Y intersection. We turned off all our lights and just waited with our windows down. About twenty minutes later, we could hear voices off in the distance, and with my night vision, I could see two individuals making their way across the cornfield. Now it was so dark out there they would never have seen us, so we just waited.

When they were about thirty yards from us, I hit the high beams, and Saterfield yelled out, "Police! Get on the ground!" And they did. Luckily, they had ditched their guns earlier when the cops had been looking for them. All we had to do was cuff them up and call the sheriff. The dispatcher asked us who we were, and we just replied, "The repo man."

We had them facedown in the wet road on that rainy night when the cops came flying up the road. They were driving so fast we thought they might run over the guys. Sometimes it is better to send in a couple of guys rather than an army.

Attack of the Wiener

We had a repo order in New Lexington, Ohio. Tod and I were after a Chevy S-10 pickup truck that was supposedly at a farm outside of town. We were in my truck and pulled up close to the farm. The house was off of the road, quite a way. It was so dark you could not see anything. Tod grabbed a Maglite and saw a reflection near the barn. We didn't want to wake anyone, so he thought he would walk up to the barn and take a look around. I stayed in the truck and only had the running lights on.

About five minutes later, all hell broke loose. All I could hear were dogs barking. I decided to turn on my headlights. I saw Tod running like a madman, elbows and knees just pumping, and he ran right past the truck and down the road. About five seconds later, five or six wiener dogs ran by the truck, right on his heels. I started laughing my ass off.

I turned the truck around and picked Tod up. The dogs had given up and were heading back to the barn. I told Tod what kind of dogs were chasing him, and all he said was that he had no idea what was chasing him. We never did find that S-10.

Information You Should Know

Now some of you might think, "Why are these guys so sneaky?" You may ask:

1. Why don't they let the debtor call the bank and make arrangements?
2. Why do they take the car and not let the person clean it out?
3. Why do they work at night a lot?

All good questions. The reason we don't want them to call the bank is that 10 percent of the time, the bank will take a payment, and we have to leave the car. We get paid $0 for this. Imagine driving fifty miles one way for no pay. Also, the debtor probably received two or three letters warning them and refused to return phone calls, and then we would get screwed.

The reason most cars are not cleaned out is that we can't knock on a door after 9:00 p.m. If the debtor does not hear me, he or she can't come out and confront me. Less confrontation is a good thing, and it's for the safety of both parties. Also, some people take forever to clean out the car and try to call the bank while doing so. Time is money.

We work a lot at night because the car is usually there. There are less dead runs if we work at night, and again, there's less confrontation at night. We would be glad to work in the day more often if we had good work addresses, but many of these people have quit their job or have been laid off from work.

Now on to my pet peeve. You would not believe how many cars I repo where the debtor has put in a thousand-dollar stereo system, new chrome wheels, and some kind of KLM air system. *Pay your car payment!* And remember, if it is attached to the car, you don't get it back.

Lancaster, Ohio

Tod and I had a run-of-the-mill repo in Lancaster, Ohio, and all the information had been verified. It was early in the day, and the car was sitting in the front yard. I hit the door, and Tod started to hook up the car. The lady came running out of the house, telling us to stop. She wanted to call the bank. They all want to call the bank, even though they have had three months to do so. Tod lifted the car, and I told the lady to clean it out. It was full of trash.

As she was cleaning it out, she called the bank and was fighting with them. The only problem was, she was cleaning it out one piece of paper at a time. She would take one item out, walk back to the front porch, lay it down, and then repeat. At this rate, we would be there all day. She had all four doors open and the trunk. We even offered to help, but she refused. She thought she was going to talk the bank into letting her keep the car. In this case, it was not going to happen.

Soon we realized this was just a stalling ploy. I told her she had ten minutes to get it done, and then we were leaving with the car. She continued to play this game. Forty minutes later, after the start of this, I told Tod to drive, and he did, with all four doors open and the trunk stuff flying everywhere. That is why, sometimes, we don't like to make contact.

Gas Station Drive-Off

Tod and I were headed to Lancaster to look for a couple of cars when we received a call from Tracy at the office. The bank had just called her and said they needed a car picked up ASAP; they were just on the phone with the debtor.

We were already in town when we got the call, and the address was just a few miles out of town. Within a few minutes, we were at the address, and the debtor was pulling out of the drive. We decided to follow her.

A few miles down the road, on State Route 33, she pulled over into a gas station. We were in my truck, so we pulled up to the pump directly behind her and waited for her to finish pumping gas. As soon as she went in to pay, Tod jumped out, looked in the car, and gave me a thumbs-up. She had left her keys in the ignition. Tod simply got in and drove off.

We headed back across the street to watch her reaction. When she came out of the station, she looked all around and then threw her purse on the ground. I think she knew what had just occurred.

We then drove the car back to the Columbus office. The bank was very happy. Apparently, the debtor was very foulmouthed to the bank representative.

Motor Home Repo

We had a mess of orders in the Mount Vernon area, so I enlisted the help of three college kids to help me pick up cars. But first, we needed to pick up a huge motor home in the Clear Fork area. The guy lived in a trailer park just outside of town.

As we pulled up to the trailer, there was no sign of the coach, but at the back of the park was an area where people parked their boats and RVs. Sure enough, it was sitting there, with a "For Sale" sign in the window. We had no keys, so we needed a plan. I decided to give the number on the sign a call and tell him I would like to look at the coach. We told him a group of us wanted to drive it on our annual fishing and hunting trips. You could tell he was excited, and he offered to show it to us. We told him we were already at the coach, and he said he would be right down.

When he arrived, I noticed he was an older gentleman in his seventies. This made me feel a little bad, but again, this repo paid $350. He got in the coach, and it fired right up. All of us were in the coach, and I asked him if I could take it for a spin. He agreed. I drove right up to his trailer and told him what was happening. He was so upset I thought he was going to have a heart attack. He went inside his trailer and got his wife and kept telling her how we tricked him. I explained that we needed to so we could get the keys. He finally calmed down after a few minutes.

The good news is, he was able to make up the back payments, and he got his RV back. The nice thing was, we took it on to Mount Vernon and used it as our base of operations for the night, and we were able to pick up three more cars. We parked it at KFC after it was closed, and we told the police it was our mobile command unit.

Another bit of information you need to know is that when we would go into a town to repo cars, we would always stop at the police department to give them a copy of our repo orders. That way, if people called in and said their car had been stolen, the cops would tell them it was up for repo. I think that at the time, we had two hours to call it in after the repo. But dropping off the orders was easier.

Reverse Repo

I was riding with Tod on this repo, and we were heading to Mount Vernon, Ohio, in Knox County. Tod and I would split Knox County. The office would send us both repos in this area. There were lots of narrow streets, and most were made of bricks, which made for a rough ride sometimes. I guess what made the streets narrow was the on-street parking.

Tod quickly found the address when we hit town around noon that day. The car was sitting in front of the given address, and I jumped out to check the VIN. We were lucky that no one was parked in front of the debtor's car. Tod simply pulled in front and started to hook it up. He had just raised the car up when the debtor ran out of the house.

Without saying a word, the debtor jumped in the driver's side of Tod's truck and took off like a bat out of hell. Tod and I just stood there for a second like a couple of idiots holding our peckers in our hands, looking at each other. A lot of people saw this happen, as many were out in their yards that day, mowing and doing family things. Tod called the police and told them what was going on, and they said they were going to send a cruiser.

As we waited for the cops, one of the neighbors yelled, "There he is! About six or seven houses down!" Tod and I took off running after him, but there was no sign of the tow truck. We soon tracked him down. He was trying to make it back to his house by running through backyards. I got to him first and was able to get him in a headlock and rode him down to the ground. Tod jumped on next to help hold him, and then to our surprise, six or seven neighbors jumped in to help us. We had run after him in a big circle, and we were only a few houses away from where it all started. Tod kept yelling at him, "Where is my truck, you asshole?"

The cops finally rolled up and told us to release him. We thought they were going to put him in cuffs and take him away, but no, the cops asked us what gave us the right to detain this man. *Are you fucking kidding me!* Even all the neighbors were trying to tell the cops what happened. I hate bad cops, and it seems that is all I run into some days.

I finally told the cops I was an officer of the court as a bail bondsman, and I had a legal order of repossession, which we had dropped off at the police department. We found out later that this cop was just too lazy and didn't want the headache of paperwork. Tod was pissed and got up in the cop's face and said, "There better not be anything wrong with my truck or transmission, because this guy was grinding gears when he took off!"

We found the truck a few streets over, with no help from Barney Fife and Gomer. The debtor couldn't figure out how to set the car on the ground once it was in the air. After a brief inspection, all was good, and we were on our way.

The cops brought no charges against this asshat. I hate bad cops.

Reno Fun

I wrote a bond in Mansfield, Ohio, for a young man who had a $5,000 bond. It was not a huge bond by any means, but I had been writing bonds for a couple of years and never let anyone skip bond on me. Well, by the time this kid's court date rolled around, he was gone. How stupid, but most criminals are stupid.

I looked all over town for this kid and finally tracked down his girlfriend, who was the cosigner on the bond. I guess he had left her in a bad way, and she had no idea where he was. I let her know she was on the hook if I didn't find him. I did hear through a couple of my informants that he was a ski bum and had been wanting to get a job in Lake Tahoe where he could give ski lessons.

Well, the next call was to his good ole mom, and it was scam time. I called and told her I was a friend from school and wanted to see my old friend. She confirmed my information that he was in Lake Tahoe, but she did not have an address. She did have a phone number. So I gave Tracy a call at the repo office, and she ran the phone number. Bingo, I had an address.

I also gave the ski resort a call and talked to the personnel office. I explained who I was and why I was calling, and they were very helpful. They pulled his application, and his address matched.

My next call was to my friend Kevin, whom I had worked with on many bonds. Kevin is a 6'5" Black man and a real smooth talker, the true ladies' man. He and I worked well together. He would take the lead in Black neighborhoods, and I would in the white neighborhoods. We always had each other's backs.

Kevin agreed to go, so off we flew to Reno. We then rented a car to go to Lake Tahoe. When we hit town, we went straight to the address and confirmed it. We then got a nearby motel and headed to the casino. Kevin taught me how to play craps that night, and with our winnings, it was off to the buffet.

The next morning, we knocked on the neighbor's door and asked him if he had seen the kid. We showed him a picture. He said he lived next door with two other guys, and then he accused them of everything, from bank robbery to the murder of Jimmy Hoffa. He was a true nutcase. The only good information he gave us was when they all got home. Apparently, they worked on the same construction crew.

Later that night, I simply knocked on the door, and one of the guys answered. They were up playing video games while our bail jumper slept. We said we were friends of his, and they pointed us to the bedroom. I slowly opened the door, and there he was, sleeping on the floor, not even in a bed. I straddled his body and took my 9 mm and tweaked his nose, saying, "Wakey, wakey." He soon opened his eyes and said, "I can't believe you came this far for me. How did you find me?"

That night, we cuffed him to the motel bed frame and went to sleep. The next morning, we headed to the airport and flew back to Ohio. He asked me several more times how we found him. I told him when we dropped him off at city jail. I told him, "Your mom gave you up." I bet that conversation went well when he saw his mom again.

The good news is, he finally got his shit together, and he owns a construction company now. Good for him.

Tailgate Buckshot

My buddy Wes McQueen wanted to go on a repo with me. I was glad to have him go. Wes played on the college basketball team, was 6'4", and could jump like a deer. We headed off to Roseville, Ohio. I remember driving by a closed-down prison on a winding road. The guard tower was spooky.

We arrived at the address—a single-wide trailer with an older Trans Am sitting in front. I told Wes, "That's our car," and I came up with a plan. Since we had keys to the car from CAC, a finance company that almost always sent keys, we were pretty confident. I told Wes I would simply drive up beside the car, and he could jump out, hop in, and take off. It was late at night, and all the lights in the trailer were off. This would be a good first repo for him.

We set the plan in motion, and it went smoothly. I dropped Wes off right beside the car, spun around, and started to drive away. As I looked back, he still had not moved, and I could hear him trying to start the car. Finally, I heard a loud bang from the exhaust, and Wes was hauling ass right behind me, dust flying everywhere.

I headed down the road and took a side street, and he followed. I hopped out and walked back to the car he was in, and he yelled, "That fucker shot at me!"

I laughed and said, "No, the car backfired."

Wes said, "Like hell it did. That fucker shot at me."

I then looked around the car, and to my disbelief, there were little dents on the ass end of the car.

Wes said, "I told you that fucker shot at me." He must have been far enough away that none of the shots penetrated the car.

I told him, "We could call the sheriff, but that has drawbacks. First, they'll impound the car for evidence, and we don't get paid. Second, we'll have to testify. Third, we'll get hung up for several hours. And fourth, the guy could say he thought his car was being stolen, which could have been true in the moment."

We decided $175 is better than the hassle. It must not have bothered Wes too much, because he never turned me down when I needed help.

Picnic Repo

Utica, Ohio, was the location on this evening, and yes, it was Tod and me. If I remember right, we were after a Pontiac Grand Am. We were about a mile or two out of town on this cool evening when we pulled up to the house.

A huge party was taking place at the time. People were in the house and out on the yard, and there were big bonfires in the backyard. They had two grills going, and people were having a great time. Cars were parked everywhere. A field to the left of the house was packed with cars. There must have been fifty cars. Our car was sitting by itself right in front of the garage. It was one of those garages that are built under the house. We had keys, which made this easy. No cars were blocking it in or anything. We just had to walk up, get in, and drive off.

I told Tod, "Let's make a bet."

His instant reply was "*No bets*. Just get the car and go."

He knew by the grin on my face that was not going to happen. I said, "You hungry?"

I hopped out of the truck and headed to the bonfire. Sure enough, there were two long tables of food, and people were helping themselves to it. I got in line like I belonged there and filled up two plates with hot dogs, hamburgers, baked beans, and the best potato salad I ever had. At the end of the table sat a cooler with pop and beer. My hands were so full that I could not bend over and grab a drink.

Just then, an older lady asked me what I needed. I thought I was busted, but she then said, "Pop or beer?"

I replied, "Two Mountain Dews, please."

She tucked them under my arm, and off I headed, back to the truck.

As I was leaving, I heard a couple walking in say, "Who is driving the tow truck?" I hurried back to the truck, sat the plates on the seat, and told Tod, "Let's get out of here." I went over to the car, and we drove off.

We stopped at the police station, reported the repo, and ate our dinner in the parking lot. Tod just sat there eating his dinner, shaking his head, saying, "You have lost your damn mind."

To this day, I still don't know what the party was for, but I did hear a lot about something going on called Swappers' Day. The next year, I found out what Swappers' Day was. It's a huge swap meet, and coon dog races are held every year. When I lived in Ohio, I made sure to go every year.

Big Mama's House

This young man thought he was going to skip bond on me. It was a $10,000 domestic violence charge. I only had one address on this guy, and that's my fault; however, most of these charges get knocked down to disorderly conduct. They pay a fine and go home.

Tod and I headed to the first address and knocked on the door, but the group of people inside refused to open it. Tod yelled, "Open, or we kick it down!" They still refused, so it was time for my size 14 to go to work. Now usually I can take a door down in one kick, but this was an apartment steel door. The first kick was unsuccessful, but the second did the job—taking the frame with it.

We did our regular routine. Tod went up to the second floor, and I dealt with the first floor, with the screaming people telling me they were calling the cops. My reply was "Please do." After a search and checking IDs, we concluded that our jumper was not present.

As we headed out of the complex, a person stopped us and said he knew where our jumper was staying. It was nearby, in one of those government-built homes for low-income families. They stick out like a sore thumb because they build them in crappy neighborhoods. We would usually wait until we saw the person, but I told Tod, "Fuck it, let's go shake them up."

We knocked on the door, and a huge, fat Black woman answered. She was wearing what I call a moo-moo dress. We asked very nicely for our jumper, and she said he was not there. We then asked to search for him, and she refused. I pushed by her, and Tod headed up the stairs. He must have scared the dude, because he jumped out of the second-floor window and hit the ground running. I could see him out the back door, and I gave chase. Luckily, he stumbled, and I was able to tackle him.

As I was putting the cuffs on him, I heard Tod yell, "Hey, I need a little help!" I turned around. This big woman had him in a bear hug, and she was yelling, "I got me one! I got me one!" I returned to the house and had to pry the woman's hands off of Tod.

Soon after, we got a call from the police, wanting to see us. We went down to the PD, and they wanted to know what laws govern us. We always carried a threefold pamphlet explaining our rights as bondsmen. From then on, Mansfield, Ohio, never gave us a problem and would even help us out from time to time.

Oh yeah, I teased Tod about that for at least a week.

Revenge on the Newark Police Department

Now after all the times Newark PD screwed with Tod and me, we had a chance for payback. We received our repo orders by fax each day. That night, we were getting ready to leave, and I thought I would check the fax machine one more time. I was glad I did. One last order came in, and it was a repo on a Newark cop. It was right about 5:00 p.m. I only lived about two or three miles from the station, so we headed there first. Newark didn't have any fenced-in lots or special parking for the police department, so if the car was there, it should be the typical hook and go.

We pulled up to the station, looked around a bit, and soon spotted our little piece of revenge. The car was pulled up to the building, with no way to get in front of it to hook it. Typically, we would hook it and drag it out, then rehook from the front, wait for the owner to come out and clean it out, and ask for the keys. But this was different, so out came the Gojaks. Gojaks are things you slip around the front wheels that hydraulically pick up the car an inch or two off the ground. You then can push the car with little effort. We spun the car around, hooked it up, and were gone. Not one person said anything to us.

A few minutes down the road, we got a call from the office. They said Newark PD requested a call from us. We just looked at each other and started laughing. We were headed for Columbus to get rid of the car. I didn't want it sitting at my house for one minute.

We decided to give them a call. The first thing they said was "You are not in any trouble, but would you guys come back to the station? Because we need something out of the car."

Now the first thing I could think of was that a gun or some type of evidence was in this car. I then asked what they needed out of the car, and I said the owner could pick up his personals in Columbus.

They said, "No, no, no, we just need one thing out of the back seat."

"What is it?" I said.

There was a long pause. Then they said, "A big box of donuts."

Sure enough, we stopped and looked, and sitting in the back seat was a huge flat box of donuts—something you would sit a sheet cake in. I really wanted to say "Fuck you and your donuts," but I didn't. We turned around, and they even had an officer waiting out front for us. We didn't even have to get out of the truck.

By the way, that box was short two cream sticks.

Taking Collateral on a Bond

Sometimes you must take collateral on a bond, something of value. This can be many things—a house or car or anything of value. Let's say someone is in jail for robbing a bank. His bond is $100,000, and Mom or Dad want to bond Junior out of jail. Well, in exchange for writing a bond to the court for $100,000, they need to come up with something of value or $100,000. In the case of a house, I would need to go over to the recorder's office and place a lien on the property. Now if Junior failed to show up for court, I would foreclose on the house and then sell it to get my money back.

During my time as a bondsman, I did several big bonds like this, and they worked out fine. On occasion, someone would come to my office who had very little collateral, but my judgment would say "I think they are good for it."

Even on a small bond—let's say the person needed a $1,000 bond. They would need to pay me $100 to write the bond, plus any court fees. If they don't have $100, I would take something of value. For instance, I have taken a drum set, a motorcycle, and even a Hot Wheels collection. I have never been burned on any one of these deals, but I did very few.

Now not to brag on myself, but no one ever skipped bond that I could not find. I had a 100 percent recovery rate. Not many bondsmen can say that.

Just Some Venting

From time to time, I will see a repo show or a bounty hunting show on TV, and all I can do is laugh. Just so you know, the show *Operation Repo* was all fiction. "Fake, fake, fake" is all I can say about that piece of garbage. I guarantee that every word in this book really happened. I swear, some of what they call TV programming these days is ridiculous. The more you look like a freak is a sure ticket to fame these days.

Another person or show is—(you fill in the blank). I won't even say his name. Ask yourself this: how bad of a bondsman must you be to dedicate yourself to a show that's been on the air for several years, showing a bondsman chasing down bail jumpers? Any bondsman with half a brain should know what bonds to write and when to walk away. If you write a bond for every dipshit who walks through the door, you deserve to be out chasing them all over town. But apparently, Hollywood thinks you are some kind of hero if you write bad bonds and then chase the person you just bonded. Just watching those guys with their paintball guns and unbuttoned shirts makes me want to find the nearest shower and get clean. The reason they carry paintball guns is that they are felons.

Airplane Repo is another one that bugs me. These shows just make our profession look bad, but I guess that some focus group out there is telling Hollywood what to put on TV. Just so you know, reality shows have very little reality in them.

Bicycle Repo

Repo a friend's car—would you do that? Would you do it for $150, and he would never know? Because if you don't, another repo man will.

By this time in my career, everyone in town knew I was the repo man. Imagine going into a restaurant, and your server is one of your repo victims. Or imagine that the guy installing a fence around your house is a guy you had put in jail for jumping bond. Not a great feeling sometimes. Well, I got a repo order on a friend at the college.

Wes was a friend of mine and helped me from time to time. I was close to him, and we also hung out a time or two. I told him about the order, and he said he would take it to the grave. He gave me his friend's address and the layout of the property, and he said the guy never took the keys out of his car. There was no garage, just a big old farmhouse on a gravel road.

Now I didn't want to take anyone with me on this one because loose lips sink ships. So my great idea was to ride my bike to his house and drive off with the car. I left the house on my Motobécane bike around 1:00 a.m. Now this was a racing bike with very skinny wheels. I had to ride about five miles, and all was well until I hit gravel roads. Ever ride a bike on a gravel road? It's not fun. I looked like a three-year-old on a bike with no training wheels. After a crash and a bit of road rash, I just decided to walk.

Now when I got close to the house, I ditched my bike in the weeds and snuck up the driveway. Sure enough, the keys were in the car, and off I went, down the road. I stopped, picked up my bike, put it in the trunk, and headed home. As soon as I arrived, I put it in the garage and taped newspapers over the windows so no one could see.

Sure enough, the next day, at basketball practice, the kid walked into the gym and asked if I got his car. Remember what a good repo man does: he improvises. I quickly came up with a story that another repo company probably got the order and that I would never do that to a friend.

Until this day, Wes has been true to his word. But I guess the cat is out of the bag now.

Pee Bath

One night, I was sitting in my bail bonds office on Main Street in downtown Mansfield, Ohio. My office was on the downtown square, right beside a bar. In fact, there were several bars on the square back then. I was finishing up some late-night paperwork with the lights down low, because all the freaks came out at night. I didn't want anybody bugging me while I worked. My windows and doors were tinted, and it was hard to see inside my office.

Sure enough, a couple of drunks were outside of my office, staggering around, fresh out of Jimmy's Bar. I could hear them talking about hitting another bar on the square, but before they left, one of them decided to pee right on my front door. As he was pissing, he was saying "Piss on the bondsman" and some other choice words about me. I was just too tired to get up and confront their drunk asses. Besides, he had no idea I was inside. They finally staggered on down the sidewalk to the next watering hole, and I continued to work.

About thirty minutes later, the same two guys were in front of my door again, and out came one guy's willy to water my door again. I didn't even know this asshole, but enough was enough. I jumped up, opened the door, and said, "What the hell, asshole?" Mr. Big Talker had trouble saying anything at that moment. I grabbed him by his arm, and when he resisted, I swept his legs. Down he went, right in his own fresh piss. His buddy took off running and ran right into one of the concrete planters the city had around the square.

I cuffed up the dipshit and called Mansfield PD, who arrived soon thereafter, but not before the Jimmy's Bar patrons came out to see the action. One guy yelled, "You don't fuck with Tom! He's an okay dude!" He was right. I had bailed a lot of people out for intoxication at that bar.

The police took the guy to jail, and soon after, I received a letter to testify. Guess what? He was a failure to appear. Imagine that.

Pat March

There came a time when I was very busy doing more bail bonds than repos. I decided to look for some help. I had bailed out a guy I really liked. His name was Pat March. He didn't commit anything too serious at the time, and I knew he was looking for some work. Come to find out, he was a former repo man for a local car lot in Mansfield. The lot had gone out of business about a year earlier, so I had Pat in for an interview.

He admitted to me that he had had a cocaine problem earlier in life, but he had gotten clean through a drug court we had in Mansfield, Ohio. He always attended meetings, and all his reports were good. Always trying to find the good in people, I gave him a shot. I told him I needed someone to run repos so I could do more bail bond work. He knew how to do repos and knew the laws governing them. We did a few together, and he did well. Soon he was on his own and doing well. I paid him on commission, so the harder he worked, the more he made.

One day, we were sitting around, talking, and somehow, in the conversation, I told him I was adopted. Years earlier, I had requested my records from the State of Ohio and found out who my birth parents were. First of all, I had the best parents in the world. You could do no better than to have George and Betty Briner as your parents. I guess that, like anyone, I was just a little curious.

Well, I told Pat the name of my birth parents, and his eyes lit up. Believe it or not, he knew them both, and he said, "I can take you to your birth mother right now."

I was in shock. I said, "Not now. I need to think about this."

He told me where she worked; she was the deli lady at a nearby convenience store.

Later that day, I drove to the store and went in to buy a pop, and sure enough, the lady behind the counter looked like me. I could tell by the nose. Later I found out I had brothers and a sister. My mom was twenty when she gave birth to me, and my father was seventeen. Later, through another friend, I found out the whole history of my family. My father was a truck driver and has a beautiful family. Both are still alive, but I have never made contact.

Pat and I worked together for some time until he wanted to partner with me, but he could not bring anything to the table. I owned the truck, rented the office space, and owned all the office equipment. I soon found out and heard that Pat was using cocaine again. I did not see any evidence of this, so I said nothing. Soon after, he wanted to borrow $1,500 to buy an engagement ring for his girlfriend. I had to say no. I asked him, "How can you get married when you don't even have $1,500?" Also, his repos were declining.

One morning, I went to my office, and the door was not locked. I checked my gun cabinet, and two of my Berettas were missing. I called Mansfield Police and told them only two people had keys—me and Pat. The cop told me, "You answered your own question." I contacted Pat, and of course, he denied it. I told him that if he could pass a polygraph, he still had a job. He never showed up for the polygraph. I can honestly say that I have tried to help several people in life with jobs, cars, money, and places to live, and I have been screwed over every time. I don't even try anymore.

A few years later, I heard Pat was doing construction work. He and his boss were giving an estimate inside a person's home one day, and on the way out, his boss saw him steal something. When Pat got in the truck, his boss punched him in the head. He died instantly.

I hope he is at peace. I will always thank him for helping me find my biological parents.

Locked-Up Semi-Truck

Ever walk up to a house and have a shotgun shoved in your face? I can assure you that it is not pleasant. I can't even remember what small town this was in, but Tod and I were after a semi-truck. Neither one of us had ever driven a semi, but what the hell, I was willing to give it a shot.

I remember walking up the walkway, and right before we got to the door, the debtor jumped out with a shotgun and put it right in my face. I didn't say a word. He then asked who we were, and I told him we were there for his truck. He lowered his gun and said that lately there had been a lot of people breaking into houses. He apologized and said he would give us the keys. He told us where his truck was and said he hoped it would start.

It was only a mile down the road, and it had a "For sale" sign in it. It was a cab-over truck. I jumped in, and after a few minutes, I figured out it was a push-button start and still needed a key. I waited for the glow plugs to warm up and then pushed the button. She growled a little and fired up. I shoved her in gear, and we were off. I noticed a red button on the side of the gearshift, and I remember thinking, *High and low range*. I was starting to get the hang of it. I remember hitting all the low-hanging branches along the tree-lined streets.

Tod soon started flashing his lights, and I pulled over. The back wheels were locked up, and I had been dragging them. The smell of rubber was everywhere, and a cloud of smoke hung in the air. I managed to get it pulled into a parking lot and gave the bank a call. They sent a wrecker the next morning.

I now know how to release brakes on a semi. In fact, Tod and I repossessed three more semi-trucks that year.

A trucker told me later that if we had gotten caught by the police driving a semi without proper paperwork, we would be in jail. That $350 order on a semi is hard to turn down.

My Dog BJ

My wife at the time, Holly, wanted to get a dog. We had a Boston terrier named Margie; she was smart, loyal, and sweet, and she loved everyone. Margie passed after thirteen years, and to this day, I still cry thinking about her.

So off to a local breeder we went, and Holly picked out one of the Bostons. I think three were left in the litter. We named him BJ—Big Jake on his papers, after John Wayne. It turned out to be fitting. BJ was not afraid of anything, anyone, or any beast. If this dog would fight a bear, smart money would be on BJ.

One time, BJ heard a dog barking in the woods. He took off like a shot, and I gave chase. On the other side of the woods was a neighborhood. The dog that was barking was a Saint Bernard. BJ had the dog on its back and had his small but mighty mouth around the neck of that Saint Bernard. BJ was nuts. He attacked my friend Mike's dog, a gentle Lab, and the little dog across the street. Now *attack* might be a little strong, because BJ never drew blood on any dog; he just wanted them to know who was boss.

Holly's little dog, whom she had wanted to love her, backfired. He was definitely my dog. The only person he ever hurt was my daughter Brittani. He bit her on the face one time when she was playing with him on the bed. She carries a small scar to this day, twenty-five years later. That day, I came close to putting my dog down, and you won't find a bigger animal lover than me.

Enough about that. One time, I had a repo in Coshocton, Ohio, and I thought I would take BJ with me for a ride. He loved to ride in the truck. We pulled up to a horse farm, and I was looking for a Ford F-150 truck. It was sitting close to the road, and in a few short minutes, I was hooked and ready to go. Just then, a man (not the debtor) rode up on a horse, asking what was happening. BJ jumped out of the truck and went after the horse. It was a male horse, and BJ was going for the low-hanging fruit, if you know what I mean. That horse started bucking and jumping all over the place. I finally got a hold of the little shit and put him back in the truck. After I apologized to the man, he rode off. BJ never went on another repo.

BJ mellowed out in time and was the perfect family pet. He went peacefully in his sleep one night. My current wife, Melanie, had a chocolate Lab named Cocoa, and she would not eat for a week after her little buddy passed away. Love you, BJ.

Warrior Tom Briner leads the distance medley.

Top left picture: Is already captioned
Right Top picture: Mom, Dad and me—ice cream time
Bottom picture: 7th Grade Basketball Team, Tod Duffner
is No. 12 and I am standing behind Tod.

Top left picture: Melanie and me at our wedding, October 4, 2003
Right picture: Taking a dance break at our wedding
Bottom picture: My beautiful wife, Melanie

Top Left Picture:—Tod's dad, Carl, and Melanie after 5k Run.
Top Right Picture: Chris Bell, me, Tod and Scott
Jones—2 mile and Distance Medley Team.
Bottom Picture: Tod winning another cross country race.

Top left picture: First wife Holly and me at family reunion
Right picture: B.J. and Brittani

Titans win one for the ages

Freshman, 36-year-old help Newark post league win

By RON WINTERMUTE
Contributing Writer

NEWARK — A little bit of youth and a little bit of maturity proved to be a winning combination for the Newark Campus men's basketball team on Wednesday night.

Freshman Brian Davis and 36-year-old Tom Briner scorched the nets in the second half to help the Titans pull away to a 107-87 Ohio Regional Campus Conference win over Ohio University-Zanesville.

"Brian is our leading scorer after four games," Newark coach John Kaminsky said. "He's not playing like a freshman. Tom loves the game and has the maturity we need. He's like an assitant coach out there."

Davis and Briner led the Titans with 21 points each. Davis tallied 17 of his total in the second half, Briner 13.

"I wasn't hitting in the first half and I was a little down," Davis said. "Coach got on me to keep shooting and got me fired up."

After trailing by 15 points with 3½ minutes left in the first half, the Pacers (0-2, 0-2) began to whittle away and trailed 46-39 at half.

"We were standing around too much and letting them get good shots," Kaminsky said. "We got flat on the other end and we weren't running our offense."

Newark held a 60-56 lead with less than 13 minutes remaing.

But Davis sparked the Titans to a 10-2 run midway through the half.

"Shane Pew, our point guard, penetrated a lot better," Davis said. "That got us going. The whole team contributes. If one of us has a bad night, someone else steps it up."

Pew dished out two of his 13 assists in the run, one to Davis and one to Matt Warthman. Davis added a free throw and a 3-pointer.

The Titans (2-2, 2-0) kept the lead around 10 points the next four minutes until Briner returned.

A Davis layup and a Briner bomb

raised the lead to 83-68. Two minutes later, Briner nailed a pair of 3s and a pair of free throws, pushing Newark near the century mark with a commanding 96-74 lead.

Eric Humphrey notched a put back to run the score to 101-83 with 1:10 left.

"We made Zanesville play man-to-man in the second half," Kaminsky said. "We pressured them and made things happen. All 10 kids got a lot of work. Some of them have been down about not starting, but I told them it's not who starts, it's who finishes."

Wes McQueen had a big first half for Newark with 11 of his 17 points. He also pulled down 8 of his game-high 14 rebounds. Pew and Troy Lewis contributed 14 points each to the Titan cause.

"They were also down about our two losses," Kaminsky said. "But we were playing 6-10 players and seven footers. Those weren't any rinky dink teams we played in Tennessee."

Titans set records in 143-96 blowout

CIRCLEVILLE — The Newark Campus men's basketball team set two team records Tuesday in trouncing host Circleville 143-96.

The first record came when they surpassed their previous best score of 142 points.

The 143-point barrage for the visitors came on the strength of 86 points in the second half after leading 57-40 at the break.

Only seven players took the floor for the Titans (9-14), and all scored in double figures.

Leading the way with a near-record was Tom Briner with 41 points, while Troy Lewis netted 28. Matt Warthman added 23 while pulling down 22 of Newark's record-breaking 63 rebounds.

Brent Urdarovski dished out 17 of the team's 33 assists.

Titans make good on free chances

NEWARK — The Newark campus men's basketball team closed out Ohio Regional Campus Conference and regular-season play with a 100-86 win over Ohio-Eastern.

The Titans led 52-40 at the intermission and maintained the differential throughout the second half.

Newark (11-15, 8-8) was greatly aided by a whopping 52 foul shots, of which they made 33. Eastern (6-13, 6-10) was not as lucky, making only 15 of 35 freebies.

Brian Davis was one of five Titan players recording double figures in the scoring column.

Davis tallied 20 points. Tom Briner added 23, Troy Lewis 10. Wes McQueen scored 15 points and grabbed 15 rebounds, Matt Warthman added 11 points and 10 boards.

Newark travels to Miami-Hamilton on Saturday to begin the ORCC state tournament against Ohio-Lancaster.

College basketball newspaper clippings

'Titan 7' succumb in finale

By CHRIS WEBER
Contributing Writer

NEWARK — Newark Campus men's basketball team simply ran out of gas — and nearly ran out of bodies.

The Titans roster, down to seven players Thursday night, made a valiant effort but came up short in losing 82-77 to Ohio University-Zanesville in the Titan Holiday Classic championship.

"One thing's for sure," OU-Zanesville coach Jeff Butler said. "Even with just seven players they kept coming at us. They play hard all the time. I think eventually they got tired legs, especially on defense. They're a good ballclub."

The Tracers (6-4) went on a 12-6 run midway through the second half to move out to a 63-58 lead. Back-to-back three-pointers from Brian Larson and Tony Hutsman proved to be the knockout punch for OU-Zanesville, improving their margin to 71-64. The Titans (7-6) made a run late, narrowing the gap to four in the final seconds, but went down to their first home loss of the season.

"They hit those two three's and we went stone cold," Newark Campus coach John Kaminsky said. "Our legs just died on us. I was real pleased with the effort of our kids, but we missed some crucial shots down the stretch."

In the first half it appeared the Newark Campus could, in fact would, pull off the win even with its diminutive roster.

Tom Briner, the Titans senior citizen at 36 years old, hit six three's in the first half — a couple coming from 25 feet out. Briner had 18 points at the half, all coming on six 3-pointers, as Newark campus took a 43-41 lead into the lockerroom at the half.

"The old man came out firing," Kaminsky said. "He's such a competitor. When he gets his feet set he can hit those shots consistently."

If the Tracers were going to have a chance at winning they would have to cool down the hot-handed Briner.

"He hit a couple of those from waaay downtown," Butler said. "We weren't even thinking about him shooting from out that far. In the second half we decided to deny him the ball and if he got the ball we wanted to force him to put it in on the floor and score on the move."

Continued on Page 7A

Basketball

Ontario's Tom Briner stuffs the ball to gather 2 points in the final seconds of the second quarter in last night's game with Plymouth. However, Ontario lost the game, 67-52. (Photo by Jim Bikar)

College and high school basketball newspaper clippings

BOB CHICK

At 30, he gives college hoops his best shot

LARGO — Tom Briner balances on the bubble of a dream, and a little bit of each of us is right there with him, trying to hang on.

Twelve years removed from high school, Briner has taken the first step to college and a degree. Yet, that's the beginning of the story, not the end; thousands return to school every year and no one stands up and cheers.

Briner, 30, wants to do it with shorts, shirt, shoes and a basketball. He wants to

Briner

earn an athletic scholarship, play four years of ball and then coach and teach.

He'll have to sell his lawn/landscape business, step away from a stable economic environment, depend largely on his wife's earnings and move to Any City, U.S.A.

Five days ago he drove from his home near Palm Harbor to Boiling Springs, N.C., for a personal tryout offered by Gardner-Webb College coach Jim Wiles. Wiles had responded to a form letter mailed to 100 schools by College Prospects of America. Intrigued, he called Briner, star of a Dunedin recreation league.

"Just wants a chance," the profile read in part. "Unusual situation." A biography followed, but a 20-point average at Ontario (Ohio) High School loses its flavor after 12 years. So what if he held the school half-mile record? Words don't score baskets; adjectives aren't translated to scholarships.

"He's better than I thought he'd be," Wiles said. "What he is doing is not a whim. He's legitimate. I believe he'll make it. ... This is a courageous young man."

All tryouts won't go this well. Wiles watched Briner hit nine of 10 three-pointers and 19 of 20 free throws.

Getting into playing shape

Briner has been jumping rope and jogging seven miles a day. He isn't in basketball shape, though, and must work on sprints and suicide drills.

Eighteen schools have responded to the letter. Bellevue College, an NAIA independent, called a dozen times. Oregon Tech opened the recruiting pitch with a call by Dan Miles. "I told him I'd be more than willing to give him a shot," said the coach of 19 years. "I've found guys up to age 35 can compete on the college level."

His proof is junior guard Nate Pyatt of Myrtle Beach, S.C., age 31, a diesel technology major and a starter on a team that has averaged 29 victories in the past four seasons. Pyatt has averaged 12 points and eight rebounds per game.

Briner has eliminated Oregon Tech and Gardner-Webb.

Briner is so heartened by the early rush he almost believes players with receding hairlines, glasses and slightly slumped shoulders are in demand. "I am playing it like a lawyer," he offered with a snappy laugh. "Some schools have told me when I get my best offer, call them back, and they'll see what they can do."

After high school, Briner turned down two partial athletic scholarships to earn $5.50 an hour in the insulation business. In 1983, unemployment drove him to Largo. He'd marry a girl he met in high school and eventually bought and sold three landscape businesses.

Mowing lawns didn't cut it

That gnawing need for something more had grabbed him a couple of years ago. Perhaps he felt he didn't want to cut seven lawns a day, as he did Monday. He thought about that while watching a television interview with David Shaffer and College Prospects of America. The agency boasts it places 93 percent of the athletes it accepts. Briner jotted down the information and shoved the paper in a drawer.

The following night at dinner, Holly Briner — college graduate, marketing major and department store assistant manager — looked her husband in the eye and said something like, "Why don't you go back to school. I know that's what you want ..."

She was right.

"This reminds me of a real-life version of 'The Natural,'" Shaffer said. Only Robert Redford, the movie hero, won major-league hearts in a script that left the theater audience cheering.

Tom Briner is not going to step on the court for Indiana or North Carolina and shoot the basket that wins the NCAA championship. Very likely he'll wind up in a small gym at a small college and earn a degree in relative quietness.

That would be worth a round of applause as well.

Story about me in Tampa Tribune, March 1, 1990

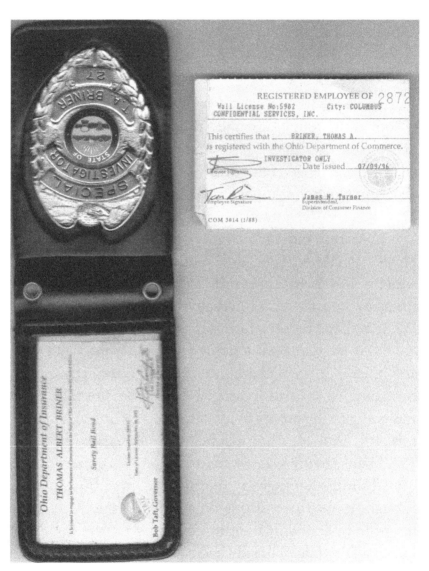

My Bail Bond's License and Private Investigator License

Our White Whale

Our white whale was a Dodge Avenger owned by a twenty-something young lady. She had addresses all over the state. I bet ten different agents were after this car. I had never heard of a Dodge Avenger, but I finally spotted one at the local fire department when I stopped in to ask for directions one day. I checked the VIN; it was not the car I was after.

I bet Tod and I ran twenty-five addresses on this car. Finally, thanks to Tracy at the office, we had the parents' address. It was in Zanesville, Ohio, only about an hour from my house. If I learned anything from bounty hunting, it is that a person always stays in touch with Mom.

Now we had been looking for this car for a full year, and it had been passed around from repo company to repo company. Now I had it again. I called Tod and told him I was going to the mom's house on Thanksgiving and getting this girl. We made our usual bet—a milkshake.

Thanksgiving was a week away, but I was patient and waited until Thanksgiving morning, about 6:00 a.m. Sure enough, it was there, sitting on a little mound by the double-wide trailer, with the sun glistening off the hood just like in a fairy tale. I already had a key cut for it, so I parked down the street, wheel lift down and ready to go. I simply walked up to the car, got in, and drove off—just that easy. The only thing I didn't do was put a spear in it.

Boy, that milkshake tasted good.

Fishing Store

In Ashland, Ohio, there is a sporting goods store that is massive, and it is named Fin Feather Fur Outfitters. I had a repo order for a huge cabin cruiser that said they were the owner.

After a little research, I found it at a marina around Port Clinton, Ohio. Luckily, this boat was not in the water. It was sitting on a trailer, and it was huge. I knew it would be quite an undertaking for me to move this boat to the auction, so I made arrangements to have a bigger wrecker tow it for me. But first, I had to clean out the personals, and it was full of coolers, rods, tons of artificial baits, life jackets, GPS systems, and anything that a well-equipped boat would have on it. My truck was so full of stuff that it looked like the Beverly Hillbillies were driving through town.

Just as I finished, the tow truck showed up, and off it went. I drove home and unloaded all the stuff in my garage. I thought for sure the owner would come and claim thousands of dollars of equipment, but no one ever did. There was not even a phone call.

Now I didn't make a lot on the repo because I had another tow service tow the boat, but the personals more than made up for that loss. An old friend of my father, who was a big fisherman at Lake Erie, made me an offer I couldn't refuse. I told you I loved personals.

That sporting goods store is still in business today, and I have even bought a couple of firearms from that store. If you are ever in Ashland, Ohio, check them out.

Stupid Stuff

Sometimes you just run into stupid people who do stupid stuff. It was Perry County again. Did I tell you I hate Perry County?

I was on my way to pick up a Chevy Silverado. I pulled up to the debtor's address, which was a broken-down trailer in the woods (surprise, surprise). I hit the door because I didn't see the truck anywhere, and I didn't want to make another trip.

The guy answered the door shirtless, and his jeans looked like rags. I told him why I was there and that I needed to pick up the truck. He pointed to a weed patch by the driveway and said, "There she sits," as he lit up a joint.

I walked over to the weed patch, and sure enough, through all the tall grassweeds and any kind of weed that will poke you, I saw it. What was once a truck was now a truck frame and three wheels. I was able to find a VIN stamped on the frame, and that was the truck.

I walked back to the pothead and said, "Where is the rest?"

After a big drag on his joint, he said, "Sold it for parts because the engine had a knock."

I was tempted to hook that thing up to my sling and haul it out, but I decided it was not worth my time. I'm not sure what the bank ever did to the guy.

Did I tell you I hate Perry County?

Stupid Stuff Again

I was off to Ashland, Ohio, to repo a four-wheeler. It sounds easy and should have been, but again, stupid people.

As soon as I arrived, I hit the door. A young man answered, and I told him why I was there. Before I could finish, he said, "*I sold it.*"

I said, "You what?"

"Again, *I sold it.*"

"But you didn't own it," I replied. "The bank owns it until you pay it off in full."

He just looked at me like I was stupid.

I asked who he sold it to, and he told me and even gave me the address. I then headed off to Perrysville, Ohio.

I pulled up to the house and was greeted by a dog with a bowling ball in its mouth—a real bowling ball! He dropped it at my feet and wanted me to play. I picked it up and gave it a toss. Just then, three guys came out of the house, followed by two more dogs that had the biggest necks I have ever seen. It had to be from carrying that bowling ball.

I told these guys why I was there, and they were pissed. One said, "I paid $800 for that wheeler."

Another said, "That ain't going anywhere."

After a back and forth for a while and me telling them about stolen property and some other bullshit I could come up with, they let me have the four-wheeler. And, boy, they were pissed at the guy who sold it to them. Before I even had it picked up, they had piled into a pickup truck and were headed to kick his ass. They stopped at the end of the drive, and one guy jumped out, ran back into the house, and returned with a baseball bat. I sure wouldn't want to be the dude in Ashland.

Lancaster T-Bird

It almost seems like any story I write starts off with "Tod and I," and this is no exception. We were looking for a T-Bird in the narrow streets of Lancaster, Ohio. Cars were parked on both sides, and there was barely enough room for my truck to fit in.

As we approached, we saw the car and a group of people standing around. We decided to circle the block, and as we approached the second time, some dude jumped in and took off in the T-Bird. They knew what was about to happen.

We followed, and he turned onto the main road and hit the gas. I knew better than to chase this guy, but I did it anyway. I had an unmarked white Chevy diesel tow truck, and it was pretty fast. I was able to keep up with him, and about four miles out of town, I pulled up beside him and yelled for him to pull over. He kept going.

I did it again, but this time, I flashed my badge. He pulled over. Now I never told him I was a cop or had any power whatsoever. I was a private investigator who had a badge that said "Investigator" on it, completely legit. What he thought was on him.

After he stopped, Tod told him to get out of the vehicle and stand at the rear of the car. We hooked up the car, and the guy asked for a ride back to town. We said sure, but that was not going to happen. He was not even the owner of the car. We got in the truck and left him standing beside the road, no shirt and no shoes. I bet he regretted running from us.

Tod's Driving Skills

Back to Perry County, and of course, this was another craphole trailer out in the woods. Except this trailer was at the bottom of a ravine. Now there was another house up top beside the road, but the truck we were looking for was down beside the trailer. And it was a monster—not as big as the ones on TV smashing cars, but close.

Tod backed down the drive and right to the rear of the truck. We had already called the sheriff to let him know what was up for tonight. Unbeknownst to us, a deputy was already on his way. I guess this guy was real trouble.

Tod had to use his sling to lift this beast, and it was hooked before they even knew we were outside. When the dude came out, he called us every name in the book and said he made his payment. They all say that. He finally said, "We'll see if you leave this property." Off to the house up the hill he headed. Tod looked at me and said, "You know what he's going for (*a gun*)."

Just as he came out of the house with a shotgun, the sheriff pulled in and confronted the guy. We could hear them yelling back and forth at each other. The guy handed the gun to the sheriff, and he waved us up the hill.

We were about halfway up when the guy stepped in front of Tod's truck and made us stop. We lost all our momentum, and the truck started to slip backward. The guy refused to move. The deputy then said, "I am getting back up." He went to his cruiser, and out came a German shepherd dog. He told the guy again to move, and this time, he did. Tod dropped it in creeper gear, and slowly but surely, we made our way up and out of the ravine.

I sure am glad that dog was there. Tod and I sent two large pizzas to the sheriff's department that night.

Did I mention that I hate Perry County?

928

Have you ever seen Chris Farley doing his skit "fat man in a little coat?" Well, how about "fat man in a Porsche 928". When I first started in the bail bonds business, I drove a Buick. You can always depend on a Buick, and in all the years of repo and the thousands of cars I have picked up, the Buicks always ran. But it was time for a change, and a Porsche 928 was a big change. So on with the story. I received a call from a bail agent in Illinois and he asked me to pick up a skip in Cleveland. Not really thinking much about it, I headed up to Cleveland and ended up in a very nice neighborhood with beautiful old homes. I didn't see my boy's car, so I decided to just go ahead and knock on the door. To my surprise an old lady in her late 70's answered the door and invited me in to talk. I asked if Big Mike was home, and she said he would be returning soon. Big Mike was written on the folder that was sent to me so that's how I referred to him as I spoke to the older lady. She asked if I was a friend, and of course, I said I was just to make things go smoothly. We chatted for a short time, and then I heard the screen door slam out on the porch and soon Big Mike appeared. Grandma said, "your friend stopped by for a visit." Mike looked confused, puzzled, and scared all at the same time. Not sure why he looked scared because this guy was huge. Imagine Chris Farley, but 8 inches taller. I asked him if we could talk outside, and he agreed. As I told him who I was, you could see the wind come out of his sails. He asked if he could get some things from the house, and I agreed. He told his grandma he needed to leave for a while, but would be back to take care of her. He just said he had to take care of some business back in Illinois. She even packed us a bag of sandwiches before we left. As we walked to the car, he looked at me and said, "you got to be fucking kidding me." Yes, that big man somehow fit in the back of that Porsche cuffed up and a bag of sandwiches on his lap. Come to find out, the bondsman in Illinois also owned a pay day loan business and Mike also owed him several hundred dollars on top of not showing up for court. All in all, it was a profitable trip. I made $800.00 for my time and met the other bondsman at the Indiana and Illinois Welcome station. Now Big Mike knows what a tin of sardines feels like.

The Penthouse Suite

Life on the run can't be fun, so never romanticise about it when you are watching a movie. I always pride myself on writing good bonds. That is why you won't see a lot of my bonds gone bad in this book. I spent most of my time tracking down people for other bondsmen. I received a call from a bondsman in Indiana wanting me to pick up a skip that had come to Mansfield, Ohio. He had the address on Park Avenue West, but not the apartment number. Now in Mansfield, a lot of landlords buy huge Victorian Houses and cut them up into apartments. This landlord made sure he used every bit of square footage he could. As I went apartment to apartment asking for my skip, I was directed up several stairways to the attic of this old house. Now this was not an apartment that you or I would consider an apartment. As I went up the steps to the tippy top of the house, I saw on the wall in black permanent marker "Penthouse" with an up arrow. As I approached the door, which was probably five feet tall, I gave it a knock. A voice inside yelled "come on in." When I opened the door, the apartment was not any taller than the door itself. Basically, it was an empty room partially drywalled with a mattress on the floor. There must have been a community bathroom somewhere in this house because the apartment was empty except for the mattress and a couple suitcases lying open on the floor. I asked for my skip by name, and he acknowledged me. I told him I had a warrant out of Indiana for his arrest and I would be transporting him to the state line where I would hand him over to his bondsman. He was in his late twenties or early thirties, and the girl he was with looked barely out of high school.

As I began explaining his options to him, he kept looking at his suitcase, then at me, then back at his suitcase. I realized there was something in that suitcase that he wanted. Being that I was hunched over in this "penthouse apartment", I knew that my movement was limited. I finally said to him, "it is not worth it," and then I repeated myself, as I watched his girlfriend grab him by the arm. He then looked like he had defeat in his eyes. I quickly cuffed him and sat him on the floor. I went over to his suitcase for a look and found a Ka-Bar knife. In case you don't know what a Ka-Bar knife is, it has a nine-inch blade and is issued to the marines as a combat knife. I am glad his girlfriend grabbed him by the arm that day. I still have that knife in my weapons collection.

Life on the run is no picnic, especially when you are living in the attic of an old Victorian house and all your possessions will fit in a suitcase.

Window Hanger

Columbus, Ohio

Kevin and I were supposed to meet at an apartment complex and pick up a girl who had skipped bond. When we were notified of the skip, he made a comment that he had seen this girl at a club a few days earlier.

We knew where she lived. She was living with her parents. I arrived first and waited for Kevin, but he was running late. I decided to hit the door and make the arrest myself. It was a second-story apartment, and there was only one entrance and exit.

The girl answered the door, and her parents had no idea she was out on bond. She asked if she could change her clothes, and I said yes. She headed to her bedroom and shut the door. I waited right outside the apartment door, on the walkway.

About five minutes had gone by when I knocked again, and this time, there was no answer. All of a sudden, I heard Kevin's voice saying, "Get your ass moving!" I looked down off the walkway, and there was Kevin with the girl, with handcuffs. I yelled down to him, "How did she get outside?"

He laughed and said, "She made a rope out of her sheets and was sliding down them from the second-story window." He just happened to be pulling into the complex when she was rappelling down the side of the building. I thought they only did that in the movies.

I sure am glad Kevin was late that day.

Licking County Mud

I received a repo order for a Ford Explorer in Licking County, Ohio. At the time, my truck was down for repairs to my wheel lift, but I still owned a car dolly that I had when I started my repossessing career. It was a nice little unit and even had a winch mounted on it.

Well, I found the address. It was out in the country, and the driveway was so long you could not even see the house. I parked my truck out on the gravel road and walked the driveway that ran through the woods. It must have been at least three-fourths of a mile long.

The house was dark, and there was no sign of the truck. However, I did see a barn a little way behind the house. As I looked around, I finally spotted my unit hidden behind the barn, tucked in behind some farm equipment. The guy was definitely trying to hide it.

I had already had a key made for it, so I jumped in and drove to get back to the driveway. There was a good-sized dip in the yard between the house and the barn, and as I drove into the dip, the truck sank axel-deep into the yard. I tried my best to get it out, but nothing worked. Soon all the lights came on in the house, and it was time for my escape.

I took off and headed back to my truck and dolly. My plan was to return later in the week and get the truck. I took off, and my car dolly, which sounded like a rattletrap on stone roads, must have been heard by the debtor. Then it hit me—the Ford Explorer had four-wheel drive, and I forgot to engage it. Boy, did I feel stupid!

Well, about 3:00 a.m., I thought I would give it another shot. Back down the drive I went, and again, all was dark in the house. This time, I engaged the 4×4 and hit the gas, and the truck moved about three feet and was stuck again. Lights came on, and I ran down the drive again.

The next day, Tracy from the office called and said the debtor wanted to give up the truck, and I could go get it. My truck's wheel lift was fixed, so I drove it instead of dragging that car dolly. When I arrived, the guy was telling me about how someone had tried to repo the truck last night, and all he heard was someone dragging something down the road. He thought he had better give it up, because he knew how sneaky repo guys were and didn't want to be at the grocery store and come out and find his truck gone. He never had a clue that I was the guy who got it stuck.

Tiffin SWAT

Tod had a repo up in Tiffin, Ohio, that was a two-car pickup, so he asked if I could run with him that evening. We never turned down a chance to work together. When you go through twelve years of school together and play every sport under the sun together, you always have a lot to discuss. I have some great friends, and some I write about in this book; however, Tod and I were on a different level.

As we made our way to Tiffin that night, I remember him talking about a cross-country course that he ran in the area. It is funny how little things stick in your head. When we arrived in town, we stopped at a little gas station, and Tod ran in and asked for directions. When he came out, he had two hoagies in his hand. If you ever want to know a great place to eat, ask a repo man.

We made our way to the address in town, and as soon as we pulled in, about six police cars pulled in at about the exact same time. Before we knew it, guns were coming out, and cops were kicking down a door. We had no idea what was happening, but within a minute or two, a cop was at Tod's door, asking why we were there. He said, "We didn't request a tow truck." Tod told them we were there for a repo, and the cop replied, "*Hold tight.*"

Soon, out came our debtor, in cuffs and shirtless, with no shoes. The officer marched him over to the truck and said, "You deal with them first." The guy was so shaken up he could barely talk. I think Tod had to explain why we were there a couple times before he understood.

At the time, only one of the cars was there. As we hooked it up, his wife pulled in with the other. She was in such a hurry to get to her husband that she left her door open, with the keys in the ignition. I just got in it and drove off.

To this day, I don't know why they arrested the guy. All I know is that he had a very bad day, and Tod had a double bagger.

AWOL

I had a repo order in Zanesville, Ohio, on an S-10 pickup truck, but the address was some army base out of state. The only other address I had was his parents in Zanesville. They were absolutely no help and refused to give up any information. I had no information. Even my ace, Tracy, could not find any information other than the army base.

So out of pure desperation, I called the base and explained why I was looking for this guy. After a few minutes, I was put in touch with his commanding officer. He went on to explain that the kid was not present and that they also were looking for him. He then said he was AWOL (absent without leave). My mind, of course, went to money, because I remember that in some old movies, when a soldier went AWOL, they had a bounty on them. I asked the officer, and he said they had quit doing that years ago; it now only applied if it was a serious crime, like murder.

He wished me good luck and said that if I found the kid, to tell him to get his ass back to base. But before he hung up, he said, "I know his girlfriend is still in high school." Finally, a lead. I remembered that back when I was in school, I would pick up my girlfriend a time or two from school.

A couple days later, I was staking out the school. I had the type of truck, the color, and the plate number. I would arrive every day around 3:00 p.m. and wait. On the second day, it paid off. The kid arrived about fifteen minutes before school let out and parked right in front of my truck. It was all coming together.

I got out of my truck, went up to his driver's side window, and introduced myself. He was wearing headphones, so he didn't hear me the first time. He took them off, and I said, "I hear you are AWOL." His door swung open, and he jumped out and put his shoulder into my midsection and tried to take me to the ground. It didn't work. He was just a little guy, and no one has ever called me little. I gave him a toss and put my knee in his back and told him I was there for the truck. He thought I was from the army, coming to take him back.

He quickly calmed down, and every word out of his mouth was "sir" this and "sir" that. He said there was nothing he wanted out of the truck except for those headphones. I hooked it up, and off I went. Before I left, I gave him a message from the commanding officer.

When I arrived home, I found a wallet in the truck. There was nothing in it, but it was nice. It had an army logo on it. I ended up carrying it for years until it wore out. Not sure if he ever went back.

Little Squealer

Utica, Ohio, was pretty close to my house in Newark, Ohio, and the orders I usually got there were good. This car was owned by a young lady in her mid-twenties, and she lived with her parents. I pulled up to the house, and the parents came out as I was getting out of my truck. The car was not there, and I told the parents why I was there. They said their daughter had moved away, and they had no idea where she went. Now how many parents don't know where their kids live? Maybe some people don't know the exact address, but all know at least the city.

The whole time I was speaking to Mom and Dad, a small boy, no older than three or four, was standing there, listening to the whole conversation. After a while, I knew that they were not going to give up their daughter's location. I wished them a good day and headed back to my truck. Just as I sat down and closed the door, that little boy walked up and yelled, "Lilly lives above the parts store in Centerburg!" Mom and Dad were in shock. You have to love the truthfulness of children.

Centerburg was only a short drive away, so off I went. Fun fact: Centerburg is the dead center of Ohio. They even have a marker in the ground. It's also the hometown of Mike Dilger. Mike was a player on the basketball team and also helped me out a time or two on repos.

I pulled up to the parts store. I think it was a NAPA store, and sure enough, there sat the car in open parking— an easy repo. The girl came out and begged me not to take it, but you know I did. I asked her if her parents had called her, and she said she had lost her phone the day before. I got lucky on this one.

Showdown

I started bounty hunting for a bondsman in Newark, Ohio. Her name was Eula Rizzo. You could never meet a nicer lady. Everyone in Newark knew Eula. She even owned a tavern in town that served the best hamburgers and onion rings. Some of her bartenders also wrote bonds, and almost all her bonds were local residents.

I think I only had to go out of state once for Eula. She had a bond out on a young guy around twenty-five years old, right about the age the kid should know better. I looked all over for this kid and finally got him to answer the phone at his mom's house. I asked for him, and he replied, "Yeah, he's not here." Something told me that voice on the phone was him.

I hopped in my car and headed to his mom's house, blowing through lights and stop signs. I was there within minutes. I parked down the street and approached on foot. When I got close, I saw someone exiting the back door with a small suitcase in hand. As I walked closer, he threw the bag in the back seat of a car a friend was driving, and they pulled out of the driveway. I calmly walked and stood in the middle of the road as he and his friend approached.

When they got close, I pulled two 9 mm Berettas out and pointed them at the windshield. I could read his lips, telling the driver to keep going and to go around. I didn't move an inch. It was the classic game of chicken, and the driver blinked. He probably thought, *I didn't do anything wrong. I am not getting shot.*

I walked up to the car and told the driver to turn off the engine and toss the keys on the ground, which he was happy to do. He was scared to death. Then I told my bail jumper to exit and lie on the ground. He also complied. Now would I have pulled the trigger? I hope not, not over a $10,000 bond. I guess if they had tried to run me over, it may have been a different story. I cuffed him up, and away we went.

I bet his buddy is still telling that story. I call that my Clint Eastwood/Dirty Harry moment. Go ahead, punk. Make my day.

Flat-Tire Fun

I was in Marion, Ohio, and having a great day finding cars. You see, Marion was not really my area; it was Tod's stomping ground. He took a vacation, probably to go hunting or fishing; he loved to do both. He would do the same in my area when I was out of town. I had already picked up a couple and stashed them at a local grocery store. My plan was to work until dark and then start transporting them to Columbus, even if I had to work all night. When you're hot, you don't want to stop.

As I worked my way through the orders, I noticed one that Tod and I had picked up before. When someone gets their car back from the bank after it's been repossessed, it is called a redemption or re-deem—at least, that is what we called it. I headed over to the house. I didn't need a map to find it, because this lady was memorable. The last time, she threw a fit and threw rocks out of her driveway at us when we were pulling away.

As I approached the house, I could see the car sitting in front, parked parallel along the road, with nothing sitting in front, so it would be an easy pickup. I swung my truck in and started to lower my wheel lift, and crazy lady made her appearance. She had one of those old-lady night coats on, along with 1950 curlers in her hair. Oh yeah, not to mention those slip-on slippers. At first, I thought she was heading over to clean it out, but that was not my luck.

She hopped in and drove off. I lifted my wheel lift, and the chase was on.

Now if you think I am going to tell you about a high-speed chase like in the movie *Bullitt* with Steve McQueen, you're wrong. She drove the speed limit and never tried once to lose me. The problem was, she would not stop. If she thought I was going to give up, she was sadly mistaken. This went on for about twenty minutes until I had enough.

Now as a repo man, you can't force someone out of a car with any physical force; they must get out on their own. In the console between the seats of my truck, I always keep a few tools, one being wire cutters. At the next stoplight, I just got out and cut her valve stem on the front wheel. Within a few seconds, her tire was flat, and she pulled off the road.

Crazy lady was very calm. She simply got out of the car and started walking home. She never said a word. She looked quite regal in her outfit as she walked away with her head held high.

Just Plain Stupid

One afternoon, I went out to the barn to check out my fax machine for repo orders. Well, it really was not a barn. When Holly and I bought our house in Newark, there was a two-story building behind the house, which I loved— more room for my stuff. It had a double garage on the bottom floor and a huge open room on top, which the previous owner had used as a chicken coop. I later turned it into an apartment, where my buddy Mike lived. We spent two days shoveling out chicken shit before we could see the floor. The ceiling was 6'2", and Mike was 6'5". He played on the college basketball team. It was very affordable, and he lived there for two years. Also, an extra $300 a month went into my pocket.

The fax machine only had one order lying on it at the time. It was fairly close to the house, and I was bored. Holly was out of town for some reason; sometimes she went to other bases to work, or it could have been that she was visiting a friend. I wanted to go get this car, but what was I supposed to do with Brittani, my three-year-old daughter? All I could think was *Easy money, easy repo. What the hell, I will take her with me.*

I put her in the truck, and off we went. Sure enough, the car was there. Before I pulled in, I told Brittani, "Okay, baby, I am going to back up to this car, hop out, and hook it up, and I want you to tell Dad if anyone comes out of the house."

Brittani replied, "Okay, Dad," and stood on the seat and kept lookout through the back window.

Luckily, everything went smoothly, but *never again*.

Okay, just one more. Mel, Brittani, and I were heading somewhere in Mansfield, probably out to dinner, when I got a call from an informant that a person I had out on bond was about to skip town. I quickly called the judge, who said it was okay if I revoked the bond.

So on the way through Mansfield, I stopped at this guy's place, and sure enough, he was packing a bag to skip town. After a brief altercation, I had him cuffed up, and we headed to the van. All he kept saying was "Come on, Tom. Come on, man. Don't take me back."

When we got to the van, I pushed him up against the fender and said, "My family is in this van, so you better not say a word to them the whole way to jail."

Brittani was probably six or seven at the time, but I had good backup. Mel would never let anything happen to her.

Okay, now *never again*.

Found Keys

I'm not sure if everything about this repo was legal, but it happened. One of the college kids and I were looking for a car in Baltimore, Ohio. When we arrived, the car was there in the drive, blocked in from the rear. We went up and hit the door. The lady answered, and I went into my standard line.

When I finished, she said, "I just made a payment yesterday." What some people don't understand is that you can make a payment, but if you're three payments behind, it makes no difference.

As I tried over and over to explain this fact to her, my buddy gave me a slight elbow to the ribs. I gave him a look, and his eyes were locked on to the TV I was standing beside. On top of the TV were the keys. Now keys are part of the car, right?

Well, this lady just kept going on and on about her payment, so I said, "Do you have a receipt?"

She said, "Yes, I do," and off she went to find it.

I just reached up, grabbed the keys, and put them in my pocket. She soon returned with her proof, and I just said, "Well, I guess I will check with the bank on Monday," giving her the illusion that she would be okay over the weekend.

A couple hours later, we returned, but the car was still blocked. My partner at the time wanted to repo a car in the worst way, so I came up with a plan. If he could get in the car and drive through the yard and over a small hill without hitting the swing set, I would give him his shot. By now, it was getting dark. He got out and looked it all over and said he could do it and cause no damage. I gave him the keys, and he drove like a pro. He didn't even leave a tire mark in the grass.

He's probably still talking about his day as a repo man. I must admit, it does make you popular at parties. "*You do what for a living?*"

Repo Dream

Every repo man or bondsman has had a dream or two about the big bust or the big find. I always thought about what I would do if I repossessed a car and found a couple million dollars in the trunk with several kilos of cocaine. Now I am not a fan of drugs, even weed, probably because it was part of my sister's downfall. I don't even drink. But if I ever found that kind of money at a young age, I would be heading for a beach where there was no extradition to the USA. Here is the best I can do for all you dreamers.

I was in Mount Vernon, Ohio, looking for a Pontiac Grand Am to repossess. The girl worked at Burger King and must have been the manager. I drove by her work and didn't see the car, but her apartment was just down the street. It was getting late. I pulled up to her apartment, and in less than two minutes, I was hooked and heading down the road.

A short way down the road, I pulled over to take a look inside. As I opened the door, I saw something sticking out under the seat. I leaned over and pulled it out. It was a bank bag—the kind that has a lock on it and needs a key to open. It was stuffed full. The sides were even bulging out. I bet there were two or three thousand dollars in that bag.

I must admit, the thought of returning the car and keeping the loot ran through my mind. No one saw me take the car. What kind of idiot leaves cash like that in a car? She was probably too lazy to drop it in the night deposit at the bank and just wanted to go home and go to bed. It was the perfect crime, but that thought only lasted about five seconds. Dang my parents for raising me right.

I took the car to the office and turned the loot in to my boss. It was three days before Burger King showed up for the money.

I never found that big score. I guess big-time drug dealers pay cash for their cars.

Pay My Bills, Woman

It is always nice to get a repo that is close to home, unless it is like this one. The man was out in his drive, washing his car, when I pulled up in my truck. He came over to me and said, "Can I help you?" I told him I was there for the car, and his reply was "You're kidding me, right?" I showed him the order, and he yelled for his wife.

She came out, and he went off on her, calling her every nasty name in the book. I think if I had not been present, he would have started beating her.

She yelled back at him, saying, "What bill do you want me to pay—the house, the car, the electric? We don't make enough money to pay them all!"

He just kept tearing into her. I thought his head was going to explode.

I hooked up the car, and when I finished, I called the Newark Police Department. I told them what occurred. I said, "I think this woman is in danger." As soon as the cops arrived, I left.

About two months later, I was driving by the man's house, and I noticed an auto detailing sign in his front yard. The sign listed all that was included in the detail. Now I had no business sticking my nose in this man's business, but I pulled in the drive. As soon as he saw me, he jokingly stepped in front of the car and said, "You're not getting this one."

When I stepped out of the truck, he walked up and gave me a hug and said, "I want to thank you. I guess I acted like a real ass the last time you were here." He said one of the police officers got him into an anger management class, and he quit drinking. He said he found a new appreciation for his wife. He even started his detail business to help make ends meet. He thanked me again for calling the police.

I hope they are still doing well.

Muskingum County

On this day, I was after a Ford F-150 outside of Zanesville, Ohio. It was a bit of a long shot, driving down to Zanesville in the middle of the day with very little info, but CAC, the finance company, did send along a key. Sometimes CAC keys worked, and sometimes they didn't.

This guy lived in a small run-down house on top of a hill, and he had some dogs staked out around the property. I'm not sure what he was doing with five or six dogs, but in that neck of the woods, I had a pretty good idea. To my surprise, the debtor was home, and the truck was sitting in front of the house.

As soon as I was making my way up the drive, he came out of the house. He was a big man, wearing bib overalls with no shirt. As I exited my truck, a dog came running up and gave me one of those low growls, but at the same time, he was wagging his tail. He was unlike the other dogs chained up around the property; he was more of a mixed breed.

As I explained to the debtor that I had to take the truck, he started bitching about how he could never have a nice truck like that one. This truck was nowhere nice, in my opinion. I would call it a farm beater. As I was hooking up the truck, this dude was pacing back and forth in the drive, talking to himself, acting like he was going to come unglued.

I finally got the truck hooked up, and I got turned around and started down the drive, when I looked in the rearview mirror and noticed him hitting the dog with a stick. The dog was all cowered down, yelping at every swat. That's when I came unglued.

I was out of my truck in a flash. As he raised his arm for another swat, I grabbed the stick and started to beat him with it. He fell in the dirt drive, and I just kept swinging. After every hit, I just kept saying, "How does it feel, asshole? How does it feel?" I then gave him a kick for good measure. The dog stayed right by my side the whole time, watching.

I walked back to my truck, opened the door, and was about to leave, when I heard the dog bark. I turned around, and he was right behind me. His eyes told a story. I said, "Do you want to go for a ride?" He jumped in my truck, and we were off.

Now as I drove away, I kept thinking, *I am going to jail for sure. Man, am I screwed.* I needed to find a home for this girl. I drove from Zanesville to Wooster just to make sure no one would find her, and I dropped her off at the shelter. The whole way of the drive, her head rested on my lap. You might wonder why I didn't keep her. Well, I already had three Boston terriers at home.

The next day, at basketball practice, a highway patrol officer walked in the gym and was looking around. I thought for sure I was getting arrested. Turns out he was there for the law enforcement class. For about a week, I thought I was headed for jail, but that dude must have never reported what I did. Even if they did find me, I would never tell where I left that dog. This is the first time I ever told this story.

You can always judge a person by how they treat animals.

Larry Bruce and Mansfield, Ohio

In 1978, Larry Bruce was accused of murdering his wife and dumping her body in the woods by the Girl Scout camp in Mansfield, Ohio. Somehow he was not convicted of the murder. Many years later, in 2002, under a cold case file, he was finally charged. Guess who the guy was that put up his bail? If you said me, you are right.

I remember that day very clearly. Larry and his family walked into my office and asked if I could help him. He looked tired and a bit weathered, and his bond was going to be $100,000. The first thing I did was run a credit check on him and a family member through our home office. I still remember when my boss called back and said, "Write that bond." I was not the most popular man in town that day. The local newspaper just referred to me as "the bondsman." Larry and his wife had the best credit score our office had ever checked. I don't think we even took collateral on the bond. When you have a credit score near 800, you're good for the money.

As Paul Harvey would say, here is the rest of the story. Larry apparently killed his wife in the bedroom of their home by smothering her while she slept. He then rolled her up in a blanket from his garage and put her body in the trunk of his car and went to work. After work, he drove to the Girl Scout camp and looked for a spot to dump her body. What he didn't know was that someone saw his

Cadillac while he was looking for the spot. How a man can run his work delivery route while his wife's body is in the trunk of his car is for only God to figure out.

Larry was able to escape justice for twenty-three-plus years before he was found guilty. He was given a fifteen-year to life sentence at Marion Correctional. I tried a few times to repo cars out of that place, and it was tough going; those guys don't play.

Larry never got out of prison. He died on April 23. A lot of people called him a playboy, gambler, child molester, and wife beater. That day in my office, he looked like a beaten-down man. I think he knew that the end of his freedom was near, and it was time to pay for his sins.

Mansfield has had its share of big murder cases over the years, and its economic situation isn't much better. In 1989, we had a doctor kill his wife and bury her in the basement of his home. His name was John Boyle, and it was national news. Boyle was sentenced to twenty years to life and received eighteen more months for abuse of a corpse. He went to prison in 1990 and was stripped of his medical license. Boyle has been denied parole two times that I know of, the last time in 2020. At the time of the murder, he had a young son named Collier. Collier went on to overcome his past and became a very successful cinematographer, and he produced a film, *A Murder in Mansfield*.

Mansfield has definitely had its share of unsolved murder cases over the years. It also does not score well in crime stats either. It has a crime rate of 47 of 1,000 residents. It has one of the highest crime rates in America, compared to all communities of all sizes. Your chance of becoming a victim of either violent crime or property crime here is 1 in 21. Mansfield needs to work on itself for sure, but all is not bad there. I have a couple of friends on the police force, and they are good Christian men.

Did you know *The Shawshank Redemption* was filmed in Mansfield, Ohio? The old prison has hosted several movies, with major stars coming to Mansfield. Mansfield also has the Mid-Ohio race car course and a carousel with hand-carved animals in the downtown area that brings in a lot of tourists. Mansfield has tried several times to revitalize the city, but business and people move to Ontario and Lexington, its neighboring communities.

Newbie

Now as I told you, from time to time, I would use college kids to help drive cars, and most of the time, they were my friends on the basketball team. One of the kids was just dying to ride along with me, so after he asked several times, I relented and said he could go. He was so excited for his big repo experience.

I had a repo in the Lancaster area, and it was a voluntary. Now voluntary repossessions are when the people give up the car, for many reasons—maybe they can't afford it, maybe the owner passed away, or the car might just be a lemon. Anyway, I contacted the owner at his home one day when I was in the Lancaster area and made arrangements to pick up the car. I was in my truck that day and already had one on the hook, so I made plans to pick his car up the next day.

As I walked back to my truck, I had an idea. I walked back up to the guy's door and asked if he would play along with a joke I had in mind. He said he was interested. I told him I had a new guy coming and wanted to give him a thrill; he was all in.

The next evening, Ron and I were off to Lancaster to pick up the car. I explained to him how I had been looking for this car and that an informant of mine told me where he hid his keys. I explained that all he had to do was get in, drive, and follow me to the auction. He then started with the questions. What if it does not start? What if the owner comes out? What if he sees me coming up the drive? What, what, what. The plan was set.

When we arrived, Ron looked at me and said he was ready. He took a deep breath, like he was holding his breath in a pool, and jumped out. He snuck up the drive all hunched over, like he was trying to disappear or hide behind something. I was sitting in the truck, laughing my ass off. As he approached the car, I saw him click on his flashlight and check the VIN, just as I told him to do. As he started the car, the owner came out of the house yelling, just as we planned. He even started running after him. Ron hit the gas, and stones flew everywhere as we drove down the road. He was beeping his horn in celebration.

About a mile down the road, I pulled over to check on him, and he was all smiles. But then the what-ifs kicked in again. What if he comes after us? What if he saw my face? Somewhere in this world, Ron is what if-ing it.

Ticket to Hell

This repo is one I really wish I could have passed on to someone else. How would you like to repo a preacher's car?

This repo was in the small town of Johnstown, Ohio. And, of course, the best time to do it was on a Sunday. What I didn't realize was that they had a big picnic after service was over. The parking lot was full of cars, and there were a lot of them. More than a hundred people were around the church, playing games, throwing a football around, and just having a good time.

I drove up and down the lines of cars, looking for my ride, a Chrysler minivan. Soon I spotted it, and I started to hook it up. Within seconds, a crowd started to form around me, asking what was going on. All I said was "I am just doing my job."

Soon the minister showed up, and you could tell he was embarrassed. I explained why I was there and apologized for doing this at the church, but his home address that I was given was no good.

All of a sudden, his congregation started opening their wallets and purses and handing me money. I explained that I was not allowed to accept cash on the bank's behalf. But they persisted again and again. Soon they had enough in an old man's hat to buy the guy a car. I told them the best I could do was hold the car in Newark until he worked it out with the bank on Monday.

Sure enough, on Monday, his car was paid off, and I was to release it to him. To stay in good graces with the Man upstairs, I delivered the car back to the minister at the church. When I was unhooking the van, several people from the church were patting me on the back and thanking me. I hope the Big Guy gives me a pass on that one.

Mad Max

How many of you have heard of a Mack R-600 Coolpower? Well, it is the type of semi that was used in the movie *Mad Max (The Road Warrior)*. Tod had a repo order for a semi in Marion, Ohio, and he gave me a call to see if I would drive it for him back to Mansfield. Of course, I said *hell yes*. I loved driving those big trucks. It gives you a sense of real power.

When we arrived at the lot where the truck was stored, we were a bit disappointed. The old girl was in pretty bad shape. It was missing a couple of tires, and it looked like people were scabbing parts off of the old girl. But as it sat there in that dirty old lot, you could tell that back in her day, she was something. Now she looked like the Mad Max truck, complete with graffiti on the side.

Soon an old man walked up to us and asked if we were there to pick it up. He was trying to jump it for us and double-checked a couple of air couplers. He couldn't believe we were going to drive the thing. But soon she came alive, and smoke was rolling through her stacks.

As we drove back to Mansfield, taking every back road we could find and trying to avoid the highway patrol, I thought about that crazy movie. We arrived back at Tod's place, and soon I was showing him how to drive a big rig. He had several acres of land, so we were basically driving it around the yard and long driveway. He later told me that he gave the kids and friends rides around the yard in the old girl.

After a few days, we had to deliver the truck to the office in Columbus, which we did, and then had to drop it at the auction. Now I haven't driven a lot of semis, but that one was definitely the most memorable.

Things You Should Know

Now in all my many years in the repo business, I have heard every excuse in the book as to why a person can't make their car payment:

1. I don't have the money.
2. I don't get paid until Friday.
3. I swear I mailed the check.
4. I just need more time.
5. I needed the money for something else.

Some of these are probably true, but can you guess who is terrible at making car payments? *Doctors*. You can't believe how many doctors just plain forget to make car payments, and their excuses are not much different.

1. Can I pay you?
2. I have been busy.
3. My wife didn't pay that?
4. That should have come out of checking.
5. Can I call the bank?

Long story short, everyone gets caught short sometimes, from a dirt-poor farmer to a doctor. Just don't take it out on the repo man.

From time to time, I get asked what is more dangerous, repossessing cars or bounty hunting. That is easy. Repossessing cars is definitely more dangerous. As you can see by this book, most of my stories are from the repo side. When you take someone's car, you take a lot from them—how to get to work, how to pick up the kids, how to go to the store, how to get another car, who to ask for money to get the car back, what the neighbors will say, how to tell my spouse, etc. I am sure you can think of even more.

When it comes to fugitive recovery, it is more of a criminal matter, not a civil matter like repossessing. I always tried to be smart when I would pick up a bail jumper. First of all, I would try to pick them up when they were alone. It is often a third party that likes to start trouble. Also, I think they know in the back of their mind that, sooner or later, someone will be coming for them. Additionally, the law is on the bondsman's side. Jumpers will run and hide, but most, in my experience, don't try to fight. Maybe I am just lucky, and most can bond out again the same day.

Loudonville, Ohio

One of my favorite places on earth when I was a kid was Loudonville, Ohio. I am sure many of you have never heard of this small town, but it is awesome. It's a small tourist town that has canoe liveries, go-karts, waterslides, restaurants, and even a zipline course. Plus, it is in the middle of Mohican Forest, where you can camp or just play in the river, which is every kid's dream. I even owned a cabin there for a short time. If not for the winter months, I would live there today.

Well, I had a repo at one of the campgrounds on Wally Road, and it was a big slide-out camper. When I arrived, the manager told me it had been abandoned for a while. He could not get the slider to go back in, and along with a couple of flat tires, it looked to be a problem. Well, filling the tires was my first job, which was no real problem until it started to pour rain.

The slider was going to be a problem. I tried every trick I knew to get that thing to move, but I had no luck at all. Finally, I just decided to tow it to Columbus. I knew that once I was on the highway, I would be okay if I stayed in the right lane. But getting there would be troublesome because Wally Road is narrow and winding and runs right beside the river. Once out of that area, there would be a lot of hills and more twists and turns.

As I started down the road, the slide-out was smacking some tree branches but caused no damage. As soon as I hit Route 3, I was stopped by the highway patrol. As he walked up to the truck, he yelled, "Did you know your slider is out?" I thought it was ticket time. But to my amazement, he offered an escort to the highway. He did give me a warning.

Once on the highway, I was stopped again, but the officer had radioed ahead; this officer would continue the escort. I have had some problems with police in the past and have worked with a few over the years and have several as friends, but these guys went out of their way to help me out. I sure appreciate their service. Thanks, guys.

Yogi

My good friend Yogi owned a towing business in Newark, Ohio. We were friends from day one. You see, when I first started repossessing cars, Yogi was my tow guy. I would drive my personal car to find a repo, and if it was at the location, I would call Yogi. He would hook it up and take it to Columbus for me. The only problem was, I only made half as much per repo.

Yogi knew everyone in town and was a great source of information. One night, we were out on a repo, and four guys came running out of an apartment and were looking to fight to keep the car. Yogi quickly picked up a chain on the back of his truck and started swinging it over his head until I had the car strapped down. I sure was glad he was with me that night.

He also did repos on the side for out-of-state banks. One car he picked up had a one-half side of beef in its trunk. That car sat in his impound yard for months before it went to auction. Boy, did they get a surprise at the auction.

Yogi was in his sixties when a nutjob tried to steal his car out of impound. Yogi jumped on the hood. That guy drove straight down Main Street before he was able to shake him off the hood. After that incident, he was never the same; it stove him up pretty good.

Yogi helped me buy my first tow truck. It was beautiful as far as tow trucks go. Later in life, my wife Melanie and

I owned a towing company in Ontario, Ohio, and Yogi would give us advice now and then.

It had been a few years since I had talked to my old friend, and I happened to be in Newark with my daughter, Brittani. I drove to his shop, and it was closed down. We walked around. Some of his trucks were still in the yard, and a few cars remained. A Newark cop pulled in and asked what we were doing. I said I was looking for Yogi. He then informed me that Yogi had died. I think he died of a broken heart after his wife passed.

You could not find better people than the Yonker family. He had a couple of kids, but I guess they didn't want to keep the business going.

Yogi was also an animal lover. One time, he even winched out a horse that was stuck in the mud. If not for him, that horse would have died. When his two dogs started having hip problems, he had a nurse come to the shop and give them ultrasound treatments every few days. You can always tell the character of a person by how they treat animals.

I hope heaven is treating you well, my friend.

A Very Bad Day

Not long after I gave up the repo and bond business, my current wife, Melanie, and I purchased a towing service. Melanie was a legal secretary in the city of Mansfield, and a damn good one. She thought it was time for her to make some money instead of making it for the attorneys, and you know my background. My best friend, Tod, even thought about joining in with us.

Well, one day, I was sitting at my desk, and my old buddy Tod walked in. He was still doing the repos and bonds, and he would stop in from time to time. On this day, he walked in and put his hand on my desk and stretched his arm out. He said, "Look at this."

I looked at his arm, and I could see the muscles twitching in it in all different places. I said, "What's going on?"

He had come from the doctor and said they were doing tests, but it could be from a tick bite. That made sense. Tod was a hunter, and he loved hunting in general—turkey hunting the most, along with fishing. His perfect day would be a day in the woods.

Tod and I had been friends since grade school. His dad coached our Little League team and was like my second dad. We ran track together and still hold records at the school today. We both loved sports cars and always wanted a Lamborghini, but we knew we could never afford one.

We could afford a Bricklin though. Remember those? We both bought one, and boy, did we think we were cool.

Tod and I did everything together—fishing and water-skiing at Pleasant Hill Lake. We even ran a triathlon together as a team and finished tenth overall. He bought rental properties, and I bought rental properties. What he would do, I would do, and vice versa. I guess we were made to be a team.

Soon after, Tod stopped back in to see me, and the doctor thought it was ALS (Lou Gehrig's disease), not a tick bite. But in true Tod fashion, he took it like a trooper. He continued to work up until he could no longer do it. Tell that to some of the lazy SOBs we have today.

ALS took its toll on Tod in a very quick way and hard fashion. He worried for his family. He was a family man; that was his true love. Tod married Angie, and Angie had two great kids; he always bragged about them. Now don't get me wrong, all mixed families have a few rough spots. I myself had a mixed family—Melanie had Charlie and Rachel when we married, and I had Brittani. Tod and I spoke often about our kids and family. See, we followed each other again.

I remember Tod telling me about his efforts to get his daughter Emily to brush her teeth or the story about Erik's pet frog. He told me Erik had a frog in a baby pool in the backyard, and one day, the frog escaped. Erik ran and got Tod, and they went over to the pool. Erik said, "Look, he's gone!" Tod then explained to him that the frog was a wild creature and that it was best for him to be free. Tod had a way with kids. Erik hung his head like he had lost his best friend and said, "I am going to miss the big guy."

Tod and Angie had a kid of their own, Ethan. You will never see a happier man than Tod that day. His dream had come true.

Angie did such a great job with Tod when he was losing control of his body. She did so much that it is hard to believe. My heart just broke for his parents, Carl and Thelma, as they were losing a son. I don't know if I could bear losing a child. Not long after, Carl and Thelma would lose another son, Carl Jr. God, please look after these people.

Soon Tod was in a wheelchair and could hardly speak. This disease is the worst, and for it to happen to an active guy like Tod, I just can't imagine what he was thinking. Later he had to go to hospice. They took great care of my friend. I remember I had to use an alphabet chart and move my finger along it so he could spell out what he was saying. We really didn't need to talk; just sitting beside my friend was enough. We watched *Dr. Phil*. He loved that show. I heard many of his quotes as we drove around, looking for cars.

One day, I was getting off work, and I was on my way over to see Tod. I was stopped at a stop sign and noticed I had a message. It was from Carl, Tod's dad. He told me that Tod had passed. I went numb. How could my old buddy be gone so quickly?

Tod had bravely battled this disease for eighteen months. He had a beautiful service at the Ontario Methodist Church, and as he would say, it was a sellout crowd.

Tod's death made me realize that life is short and that we are never guaranteed tomorrow. He is why I am living in Florida today and why I am semi-retired. Life *is* short.

You can't live your life through your children. You teach them well and let them figure life out for themselves. Set an example, go to a beach, travel, eat good food, and make lots of friends. As Tod would say, you will want a sellout crowd one day.

I think of you every day.

Miss you, buddy.

Top picture: My daughters, Brittani and Rachel
Middle picture: My son, Charlie, wife, Tiffany
and grandchildren, Cael and Scarlett
Bottom picture: Me, Brittani and B.J. in 1996.

My 1975 Bricklin and Tod's Bricklin was white

Tod Owen Duffner

ONTARIO — Tod Owen Duffner, 47, died Tuesday, May 20, 2008, at Hospice House of Hospice of North Central Ohio, Ashland.

He courageously battled ALS for 18 months.

Tod was born March 15, 1961, in Mansfield to Carl and Thelma Duffner. He was employed for ten years at Confidential Services, served as a bail bondsman, and prior to that worked as an auto body refinishing technician at G and M Body Shop. He was a member of the Ontario United Methodist Church.

Duffner

Duffner

Tod graduated from Ontario High School in 1979. He was an outstanding distance runner in track and a state finalist in cross country.

Tod will be remembered for the love he had for the simple life. Spending time with his family and being outdoors brought him the most joy. He was an enthusiastic hunter and fisherman, with a particular passion for turkey hunting. He enjoyed sports of all kinds, and when he was not formally coaching, he was always eager to play a family game of basketball, baseball, football, volleyball, or swimming pool races.

Tod adored the children in his life. He had a gift of making them all feel important and special. Tod was a loving and devoted husband, father, son, brother, uncle and a good friend to many.

Survivors include his wife Angie; children, Emily, Erik and Ethan Tod; parents, Carl and Thelma Duffner; brothers and sisters-in-law, Carl and Mindy Duffner, Bruce Duffner, and Brett and Laura Duffner; his father- and mother-in-law, Frank and Debra Lucanegro; brothers-and sisters-in-law, Anthony and Allison Lucanegro, Teresa and Brian Stough, and Tracy and Terance Trammell; 10 nieces and nephews; a large extended family; and a large circle of friends.

The service to celebrate God's gift of the life of Tod Duffner will be held Friday, May 23, 2008 at 7 p.m. in The Ontario United Methodist Church, 3540 Park Avenue West, Mansfield. Pastor David Case will officiate. The family will receive friends in the fellowship hall of the church immediately following the service.

The Marion Avenue Snyder Funeral Home (Former Finefrock Funeral Home) is honored to serve the Duffner Family.

In lieu of flowers, the family prefers contributions in Tod's memory be made to benefit Tod's children or to fund finding a cure for ALS through projectALS.org, and may be made at the service, or through the funeral home: Snyder Funeral Home, 350 Marion Ave., Mansfield, OH 44903.

Snyder Funeral Homes

Condolences may be made to the Duffner Family online at: www.snyderfuneralhomes.com.

Tod's Obituary

About the Author

Tom Briner, who came from a middle-class family in North Central, Ohio, was unsure of the path he should follow in life. He knew he wanted to be his own boss and desired the freedom to make his own choices and not work a nine-to-five. After going through various jobs, which included factory work, general labor, landscaping, and security, Tom decided to return to college and was offered basketball scholarships at the age of thirty, before landing in Newark, Ohio.

In the early nineties, in need of a job and while playing college basketball, Tom Briner talked his way into an auto repossession job. Within a short time, he was one of the best in the business and on his way to becoming a bounty hunter. After recruiting his best friend, Tod Duffner, they traveled the state of Ohio and the country, repossessing cars and tracking down bail jumpers.

Tod would contract Lou Gehrig's disease and would go from a healthy young man to being disabled in months. The following short stories will make you laugh and cry at their adventures. Tom and Tod's crazy life will give you an inside look at the real world of a repo man and bondsman.

This book is dedicated to Tom's best friend, Tod Duffner, and his family.

CPSIA information can be obtained
at www.ICGtesting.com
Printed in the USA
LVHW091645200322
713918LV00004B/156